ON BOXING

ALSO BY JOYCE CAROL OATES

Joyce Carol Oates

ON BOXING

With photographs by John Ranard

AN  BOOK

HARPER  PERENNIAL

NEW YORK • LONDON • TORONTO • SYDNEY

HARPER ● PERENNIAL

For the contenders . . .

CONTENTS

CONTENTS

PREFACE

No other subject is, for the writer, so intensely personal as boxing. To write about boxing is to write about oneself—however elliptically, and unintentionally. And to write about boxing is to be forced to contemplate not only boxing, but the perimeters of civilization—what it is, or should be, to be "human."

When I was writing *On Boxing*, in the grip of a curious, inexplicable compulsion, from February 1985 (when I drafted a short story titled "Golden Gloves"—I never understood why) to spring 1987, it happened that I was riding the crest, without knowing it, of a triumphant era in this turbulent and always precarious American "sport." The great, inimitable Muhammad Ali had retired, but Larry Holmes was an estimable, intrepid heavyweight champion. Marvin Hagler was a brilliant middleweight champion. The ingenious Sugar Ray Leonard, recently retired, was due soon to return—with unexpectedly spectacular results. There was Michael Spinks, there was Thomas Hearns, there was the buttery-smooth and seemingly invincible Donald Curry. There was, seemingly forever, Roberto Durán. There was the beloved Irish featherweight champion Barry McGuigan. And a Cus D'Amato-trained young man named Mike Tyson, whose first professional fight was in March 1985, was rapidly ascending the ranks of the heavyweight division by knock-outs. Like the legendary Harry Greb, Tyson seemed to be training by fighting, every two or three weeks, indefatigably. Tyson's career was so meteoric, and so self-consuming, that it has seemed as much moral exemplum as sports history: beginning in public glory, ending in public shame. (If, in fact, Tyson's career, after his conviction on charges of rape in February 1992, has ended.)

Much has changed in boxing since that time, though it has been hardly a decade. Virtually all of the reigning boxers have disappeared. The enormous purses of the 1980's—the theme of an entire chapter of *On Boxing*—have been multiplied tenfold for heavyweight title fights. The sport seems in crisis, its best practitioners no less than its most dubious contaminated by association with fixed fights, manipulated judges, questionable referees. Demands for its abolition are made, indignation is aroused, well-argued editorials are printed, deals continue to be made, boxers continue to be "managed." Occasionally there is a boxing match that, in its demonstration of skill, courage, intelligence, hope, seems to redeem the sport—or almost. Perhaps boxing has always been in crisis, a sport *of* crisis.

Without doubt, it is our most dramatically "masculine" sport, and our most dramatically "self-destructive" sport. In this, for some of us, its abiding interest lies.

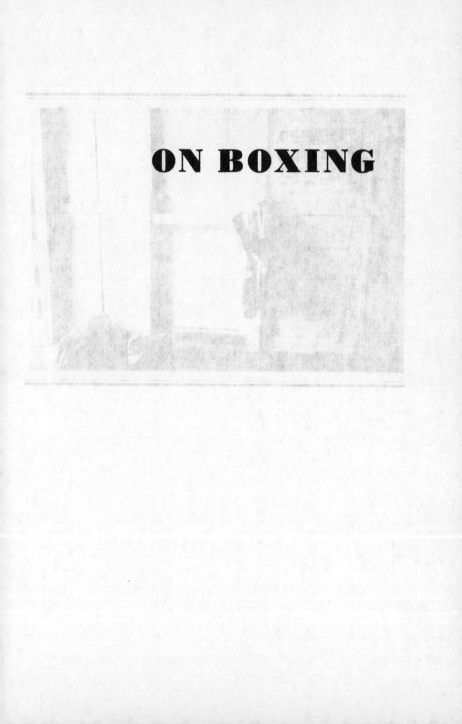

ON BOXING

It's a terrible sport, but it's a sport . . . .
the fight for survival is the fight.
—ROCKY GRAZIANO,
former middleweight champion of the world

They are young welterweight boxers so evenly matched they might be twins, though one has a redhead's pallor and the other is a dusky-skinned Hispanic. Circling each other in the ring, beneath the glaring lights, trying jabs, tentative left hooks, right crosses that dissolve in mid-air or turn into harmless slaps. How to get inside! How to press an advantage, score a point or two, land a single punch! It seems they have forgotten all they've been trained to do and the Madison Square Garden fight crowd is getting noisy, derisive, impatient. Time is running out. "Those two—what'd they do, wake up this morning and decide they were boxers?" a man behind me says in disgust. (He's dark, nattily dressed, neat-trimmed moustache and tinted glasses. A sophisticated fight fan. Knows all the answers. Two hours later he will be screaming, "Tommy! Tommy! Tommy!" over and over in a paroxysm of grief as, on the giant closed-circuit television screen lowered over the ring, middleweight champion Marvelous Marvin Hagler batters his brash challenger Thomas Hearns into insensibility.)

The young welterweights are surely conscious of the chorus of jeers, boos, and catcalls in this great cavernous space reaching up into the cheap twenty-dollar seats in the balconies amid the constant milling of people in the aisles, the commingled smells of hotdogs, beer, cigarette and cigar smoke, hair oil. But they are locked desperately together in their futile match—circling, "dancing," jabbing, slapping, clinching—now a flurry of light blows, clumsy footwork, yet another sweaty stumbling despairing clinch into the ropes that provokes a fresh wave of derision as the referee helps them apart. Why are they here in the Garden of all places, each fighting, it seems, his first professional fight? Neither wants to hurt the other—neither is angry at the other. When the bell sounds at the end of the fourth and final round the crowd boos a little louder. The Hispanic boy, silky yellow shorts, damp frizzy floating hair, strides about his corner of the ring with his gloved hand aloft—not in defiance of the boos which increase in response to his gesture, or even in acknowledgment of them. It's just something he's doing, something he has seen older boxers do, he's saying *I'm here, I made it, I did it.*

When the decision is announced as a draw the crowd's derision increases in volume. "Get out of the ring!" "Assholes!" "Go home!" Contemptuous male laughter follows the boys up the aisle in their robes, towels about their heads, sweating, breathless. Why had *they* thought they were boxers?

How can you enjoy so brutal a sport, people sometimes ask me.

Or pointedly don't ask.

And it's too complex to answer. In any case I don't
"enjoy" boxing in the usual sense of the word, and never
have; boxing isn't invariably "brutal"; and I don't think
of it as a "sport."

Nor can I think of boxing in writerly terms as a
metaphor for something else. No one whose interest began
as mine did in childhood—as an offshoot of my father's
interest—is likely to think of boxing as a symbol of something beyond itself, as if its uniqueness were merely an
abbreviation, or iconographic; though I can entertain the
proposition that life is a metaphor for boxing—for one of
those bouts that go on and on, round following round,
jabs, missed punches, clinches, nothing determined, again
the bell and again and you and your opponent so evenly
matched it's impossible not to see that your opponent *is*
you: and why this struggle on an elevated platform en-
closed by ropes as in a pen beneath hot crude pitiless
lights in the presence of an impatient crowd?—that sort
of hellish-writerly metaphor. Life *is* like boxing in many
unsettling respects. But boxing is only like boxing.

For if you have seen five hundred boxing matches
you have seen five hundred boxing matches and their
common denominator, which certainly exists, is not of pri-

mary interest to you. "If the Host is only a symbol," as the Catholic writer Flannery O'Connor once remarked, "I'd say the hell with it."

I am a fighter who walks, talks, and thinks fighting, but I try not to look like it.
—*MARVELOUS MARVIN HAGLER,*
middleweight champion of the world

Like a dancer, a boxer "is" his body, and is totally identified with it. And the body is identified with a certain weight:

HEAVYWEIGHT—no weight limit
CRUISERWEIGHT—not over 195 pounds
LIGHT HEAVYWEIGHT—not over 175 pounds
MIDDLEWEIGHT—not over 160 pounds
JUNIOR MIDDLEWEIGHT—not over 154 pounds
WELTERWEIGHT—not over 147 pounds
JUNIOR WELTERWEIGHT—not over 140 pounds
LIGHTWEIGHT—not over 135 pounds
JUNIOR LIGHTWEIGHT—not over 130 pounds
FEATHERWEIGHT—not over 126 pounds
JUNIOR FEATHERWEIGHT—not over 122 pounds

BANTAMWEIGHT—not over 118 pounds
FLYWEIGHT—not over 112 pounds

Though the old truism "A good big man will always beat a good little man" has been disproved any number of times (most recently by Michael Spinks in his victory over Larry Holmes) it is usually the case that a boxer invites disaster by fighting out of his weight division: he can "move up" but very likely he can't "bring his punch with him." Where at one time the distinctions between weight were fairly crude (paralleling life's unfairness—the mismatches of most battles outside the ring) boxing promoters and commissions have created a truly Byzantine hierarchy of weights to regulate present-day fights. In theory, the finely calibrated divisions were created to prevent mismatches; in practice, they have the felicitous effect of creating many more "champions" and many more lucrative "title" shots. So it is, an ambitious boxer in our time hopes not only to be a champion but to be a great champion—an immortal; he may try for multiple titles, like Sugar Ray Robinson (world welter- and middleweight champion who tried, and failed, to win the light-heavyweight title from Joey Maxim), Sugar Ray Leonard (world welter- and junior-middleweight champion), Roberto Durán (world light-, welter- and light-middleweight champion who tried, and failed, to move up to middleweight), Alexis Arguello (world featherweight, junior lightweight, and lightweight champion who hoped for a junior welterweight title before his recent retirement).

In order to make his weight the boxer may resort to fasting or vigorous exercise so close to fight time that he risks serious injury: like, most recently, WBA bantamweight champion Richie Sandoval who lost ten pounds in a short period of time and, in his match with Gaby Canizales in March 1986, nearly lost his life as a consequence. When Michael Spinks made boxing history in September 1985 by becoming the first light-heavyweight to win the heavyweight title, as much excited media attention was paid to Spinks's body as to his boxing. For Spinks had accomplished what constituted a *tour de force* of the physical—with the help of his trainer and nutritionist he had created for himself a true heavyweight's body: two hundred pounds of solid muscle. And though his opponent Larry Holmes outweighed him by twenty-odd pounds it scarcely mattered since Spinks had not merely gained weight, he had become a "new" body. And he sustained this remarkable new body for his title defense against Holmes, which he also won. Boxing's fanaticism can go no further.

Why are you a boxer, Irish featherweight champion Barry McGuigan was asked. He said: "I can't be a poet. I can't tell stories . . ."

E ach boxing match is a story—a unique and highly condensed drama without words. Even when nothing sensational happens: then the drama is "merely" psychological. Boxers are there to establish an absolute experience, a public accounting of the outermost limits of their beings; they will know, as few of us can know of ourselves, what physical and psychic power they possess—of how much, or how little, they are capable. To enter the ring near-naked and to risk one's life is to make of one's audience voyeurs of a kind: boxing is so intimate. It is to ease out of sanity's consciousness and into another, difficult to name. It is to risk, and sometimes to realize, the agony of which *agon* (Greek, "contest") is the root.

In the boxing ring there are two principal players, overseen by a shadowy third. The ceremonial ringing of the bell is a summoning to full wakefulness for both boxers and spectators. It sets into motion, too, the authority of Time.

The boxers will bring to the fight everything that is themselves, and everything will be exposed—including secrets about themselves they cannot fully realize. The physical self, the maleness, one might say, underlying the "self." There are boxers possessed of such remarkable intuition, such uncanny prescience, one would think they were somehow recalling their fights, not fighting them as we watch. There are boxers who perform skillfully, but mechanically, who cannot improvise in response to another's alteration of strategy; there are boxers performing at the peak of their talent who come to realize, mid-fight, that it will not be enough; there are boxers—including great champions—whose careers end abruptly, and irrevocably, as we watch. There has been at least one boxer possessed of an extraordinary and disquieting awareness not only of his opponent's every move and anticipated move but of the audience's keenest shifts in mood as well, for which he seems to have felt personally responsible—Cassius Clay / Muhammad Ali, of course. "The Sweet Science of Bruising" celebrates the physicality of men even as it dramatizes the limitations, sometimes tragic, more often poignant, of the physical. Though male spectators identify with boxers no boxer behaves like a "normal" man when he is in the ring and no combination of blows is "natural." All is style.

Every talent must unfold itself in fighting. So Nietzsche speaks of the Hellenic past, the history of the "contest"—athletic, and otherwise—by which Greek youths were educated into Greek citizenry. Without the ferocity of competition, without, even, "envy, jealousy, and ambition" in the contest, the Hellenic city, like the Hellenic man, degenerated. If death is a risk, death is also the prize—for the winning athlete.

In the boxing ring, even in our greatly humanized times, death is always a possibility—which is why some of us prefer to watch films or tapes of fights already past, already defined as history. Or, in some instances, art. (Though to prepare for writing this mosaic-like essay I saw tapes of two infamous "death" fights of recent times: the Lupe Pintor–Johnny Owen bantamweight match of 1982, and the Ray Mancini–Duk Koo-Kim lightweight match of the same year. In both instances the boxers died as a consequence of their astonishing resilience and apparent indefatigability—their "heart," as it's known in boxing circles.) Most of the time, however, death in the ring is extremely unlikely; a statistically rare possibility like your possible death tomorrow morning in an automobile accident or in next month's headlined airline disaster or in a freak accident involving a fall on the stairs or in the bathtub, a skull fracture, subarachnoid hemorrhage. Spectators at "death" fights often claim afterward that what happened simply seemed to happen—unpredictably, in a sense accidentally. Only in retrospect does death appear to have been inevitable.

If a boxing match is a story it is an always wayward story, one in which anything can happen. And in a matter of seconds. Split seconds! (Muhammad Ali boasted that he could throw a punch faster than the eye could follow, and he may have been right.) In no other sport can so much take place in so brief a period of time, and so irrevocably.

Because a boxing match is a story without words, this doesn't mean that it has no text or no language, that it is somehow "brute," "primitive," "inarticulate," only that the text is improvised in action; the language a dialogue between the boxers of the most refined sort (one might say, as much neurological as psychological: a dialogue of split-second reflexes) in a joint response to the mysterious will of the audience which is always that the fight be a worthy one so that the crude paraphernalia of the setting —ring, lights, ropes, stained canvas, the staring onlookers themselves—be erased, forgotten. (As in the theater or the church, settings are erased by way, ideally, of transcendent action.) Ringside announcers give to the wordless spectacle a narrative unity, yet boxing as performance is more clearly akin to dance or music than narrative.

To turn from an ordinary preliminary match to a "Fight of the Century" like those between Joe Louis and Billy Conn, Joe Frazier and Muhammad Ali, Marvin Hagler and Thomas Hearns is to turn from listening or half-listening to a guitar being idly plucked to hearing Bach's *Well-Tempered Clavier* perfectly executed, and that too is part of the story's mystery: so much happens so swiftly and with such heart-stopping subtlety you cannot absorb it except to know that something profound is happening and it is happening in a place beyond words.

*I try to catch my opponent on the tip of his nose
because I try to punch the bone into his brain.*
—MIKE TYSON,

Boxing's claim is that it is superior to life in that it is, ideally, superior to all accident. It contains nothing that is not fully willed.

The boxer meets an opponent who is a dream-distortion of himself in the sense that his weaknesses, his capacity to fail and to be seriously hurt, his intellectual miscalculations—all can be interpreted as strengths belonging to the Other; the parameters of his private being are nothing less than boundless assertions of the Other's self. This is dream, or nightmare: my strengths are not fully my own, but my opponent's weaknesses; my failure is not fully my own, but my opponent's triumph. He is my shadow-self, not my (mere) shadow. The boxing match as "serious, complete, and of a certain magnitude"—to refer to Aristotle's definition of tragedy—is an event that necessarily subsumes both boxers, as any ceremony subsumes its participants. (Which is why one can say, for instance, that the greatest fight of Muhammad Ali's career was one of the few fights Ali lost—the first heroic match with Frazier.)

The old boxing adage—a truism surely untrue—that you cannot be knocked out if you see the blow coming, and if you *will* yourself not to be knocked out, has its subtler, more daunting significance: nothing that happens to the boxer in the ring, including death—"his" death—is not of his own will or failure of will. The suggestion is of a world-model in which we are humanly responsible not only for our own acts but for those performed against us.

Which is why, though springing from life, boxing is not a metaphor for life but a unique, closed, self-referential world, obliquely akin to those severe religions in which the individual is both "free" and "determined"—in one sense possessed of a will tantamount to God's, in another totally helpless. The Puritan sensibility would have understood a mouth filling with blood, an eye popped out of its socket—fit punishment for an instant's negligence.

A boxing trainer's most difficult task is said to be to persuade a young boxer to get up and continue fighting after he has been knocked down. And if the boxer has been knocked down by a blow he hadn't seen coming—which is usually the case—how can he hope to protect himself from being knocked down again? and again? The invisible blow is after all—invisible.

"Normal" behavior in the ring would be unbearable to watch, deeply shameful: for "normal" beings share with all living creatures the instinct to persevere, as Spi-

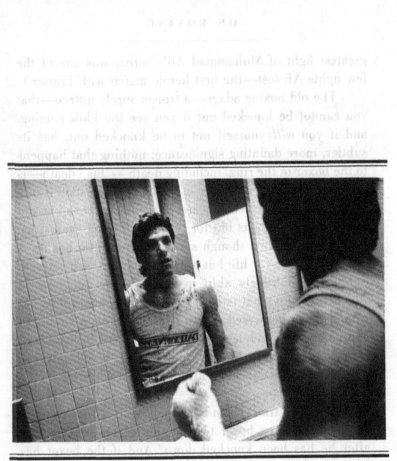

been knocked down by a blow he hadn't seen coming—which is usually the case—how can he hope to protect himself from being knocked down again? and again? The invisible blow is after all—invisible.

"Normal" behavior in the ring would be unbearable to watch, deeply shameful for "normal" beings share with all living creatures the instinct to persevere, as Spinoza said, in their own being. The boxer must somehow learn, by what effort of will non-boxers surely cannot guess, to inhibit his own instinct for survival; he must learn to exert his "will" over his merely human and animal impulses, not only to flee pain but to flee the unknown. In psychic terms this sounds like magic. Levitation. Sanity turned inside out, "madness" revealed as a higher and more pragmatic form of sanity.

The fighters in the ring are time-bound—surely nothing is so excruciatingly long as a fiercely contested three-minute round—but the fight itself is timeless. In a sense it becomes all fights, as the boxers are all boxers. By way of films, tapes, and photographs it quickly becomes history for us, even, at times, art. Time, like the possibility of death, is the invisible adversary of which the boxers—and the referee, the seconds, the spectators—are keenly aware. When a boxer is "knocked out" it does not mean, as it's commonly thought, that he has been knocked unconscious, or even incapacitated; it means rather more poetically that he has been knocked out of Time. (The referee's dramatic count of ten constitutes a metaphysical parenthesis of a kind through which the fallen boxer must penetrate if he hopes to continue in Time.) There are in a sense two dimensions of Time abruptly operant: while the standing boxer is *in time* the fallen boxer is *out of time.* Counted out, he is counted "dead"—in symbolic mimicry of the sport's ancient tradition in which he would very likely be dead. (Though, as we may recall, the canny Romans reserved for themselves as spectators the death blow itself: the triumphant gladiator was obliged to wait for a directive from outside the arena before he finished off his opponent.)

If boxing is a sport it is the most tragic of all sports because more than any human activity it consumes the very excellence it displays—its drama is this very consumption. To expend oneself in fighting the greatest fight of one's life is to begin by necessity the downward turn that next time may be a plunge, an abrupt fall into the abyss. *I am the greatest* says Muhammad Ali. *I am the greatest* says Marvelous Marvin Hagler. You always think you're going to win, Jack Dempsey wryly observed in his old age, otherwise you couldn't fight at all. The punishment—to the body, the brain, the spirit—a man must endure to become even a moderately good boxer is inconceivable to most of us whose idea of personal risk is largely ego-related or emotional. But the punishment as it begins to show in even a young and vigorous boxer is closely gauged by his rivals, who are waiting for him to slip. (After junior-welterweight champion Aaron Pryor won a lackluster fight last year a younger boxer in his weight division, interviewed at ringside, said with a smile: "My mouth is watering." And there was twenty-nine-year-old Billy Costello's bold statement—"If I can't beat an old man [of thirty-three] then I should retire"—shortly before his bout with Alexis Arguello, in which he was knocked out in an early round.)

In the ring, boxers inhabit a curious sort of "slow" time—amateurs never box beyond three rounds, and for most amateurs those nine minutes are exhausting—while outside the ring they inhabit an alarmingly accelerated time. A twenty-three-year-old boxer is no longer young in the sense in which a twenty-three-year-old man is young; a thirty-five-year-old is frankly old. (Which is why Muhammad Ali made a tragic mistake in continuing his career after he had lost his title for the second time—to come out of retirement, aged thirty-eight, to fight Larry Holmes; and why Holmes made a similar mistake, years later, in needlessly exposing himself to injury, as well as professional embarrassment, by meeting with the light-heavyweight champion Michael Spinks. The victory of the thirty-seven-year-old Jersey Joe Walcott over the thirty-year-old Ezzard Charles, for the heavyweight title in 1951, is *sui generis*. And Archie Moore is *sui generis*.) All athletes age rapidly but none so rapidly and so visibly as the boxer.

So it is, the experience of watching great fighters of the past is radically different from having seen them perform when they were reigning champions. Jack Johnson, Jack Dempsey, Joe Louis, Sugar Ray Robinson, Rocky Marciano, Muhammad Ali, Joe Frazier—as spectators we know not only how a fight but how a career ends. The trajectory not merely of ten or fifteen rounds but that of an entire life . . .

Everything that man esteems
Endures a moment or a day.
Love's pleasure drives his love away,

The painter's brush consumes his dreams;
The herald's cry, the soldier's tread
Exhaust his glory and his might:
Whatever flames upon the night
Man's own resinous heart has fed.

—WILLIAM BUTLER YEATS, *from "The Resurrection"*

When I see blood, I become a bull.
—*MARVIN HAGLER*

I have no difficulty justifying boxing as a sport because I have never thought of it as a sport.

There is nothing fundamentally playful about it; nothing that seems to belong to daylight, to pleasure. At its moments of greatest intensity it seems to contain so complete and so powerful an image of life—life's beauty, vulnerability, despair, incalculable and often self-destructive courage—that boxing *is* life, and hardly a mere game. During a superior boxing match (Ali-Frazier I, for instance) we are deeply moved by the body's communion with itself by way of another's intransigent flesh. The body's dialogue with its shadow-self—or Death. Baseball,

· 18 ·

football, basketball—these quintessentially American pastimes are recognizably sports because they involve play: they are games. One *plays* football, one doesn't *play* boxing.

Observing team sports, teams of adult men, one sees how men are children in the most felicitous sense of the word. But boxing in its elemental ferocity cannot be assimilated into childhood. (Though very young men box, even professionally, and many world champions began boxing in their early or mid-teens. By the time he was sixteen Jack Dempsey, rootless and adrift in the West, was fighting for small sums of money in unrefereed saloon fights in which—in the natural course of things—he might have been killed.) Spectators at public games derive much of their pleasure from reliving the communal emotions of childhood but spectators at boxing matches relive the murderous infancy of the race. Hence the occasional savagery of boxing crowds—the crowd, largely Hispanic, that cheered as the Welshman Johnny Owen was pounded into insensibility by the Mexican bantamweight champion Lupe Pintor, for instance—and the excitement when a man begins to seriously bleed.

Marvelous Marvin Hagler, speaking of blood, is speaking, of course, of his own.

Considered in the abstract the boxing ring is an altar of sorts, one of those legendary spaces where the laws of a nation are suspended: inside the ropes, during an officially regulated three-minute round, a man may be killed at his opponent's hands but he cannot be legally murdered. Box-

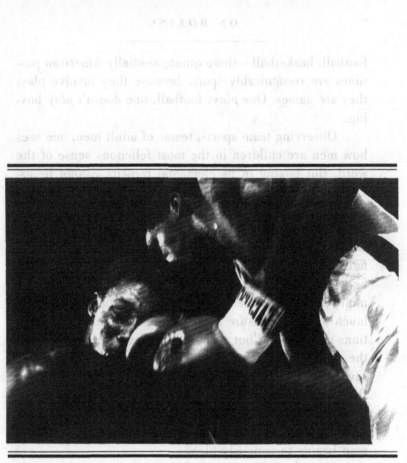

Marvelous Marvin Hagler, speaking of blood, is speaking, of course, of his own.

Considered in the abstract the boxing ring is an altar of sorts, one of those legendary spaces where the laws of a nation are suspended: inside the ropes, during an officially regulated three-minute round, a man may be killed at his opponent's hands but he cannot be legally murdered. Boxing inhabits a sacred space predating civilization; or, to use D. H. Lawrence's phrase, before God was love. If it suggests a savage ceremony or a rite of atonement it also suggests the futility of such gestures. For what possible atonement is the fight waged if it must shortly be waged again . . . and again? The boxing match is the very image, the more terrifying for being so stylized, of mankind's collective aggression; its ongoing historical madness.

I hate to say it, but it's true—
I only like it better when pain comes.
—FRANK *"THE ANIMAL"* FLETCHER,
former middleweight contender

Years ago in the early 1950s when my father first took me to a Golden Gloves boxing tournament in Buffalo, New York, I asked him why the boys wanted to fight one another, why they were willing to get hurt. As if it were an explanation my father said, "Boxers don't feel pain quite the way we do."

Pain, in the proper context, is something other than pain.

Consider: Gene Tunney's single defeat in a thirteen-year career of great distinction was to a notorious fighter named Harry Greb who seems to have been, judging from boxing lore, the dirtiest fighter in history. Greb was infamous for his fouls—low blows, butting, "holding and hitting," rubbing his laces against an opponent's eyes, routine thumbing—as well as for a frenzied boxing style in which blows were thrown from all directions. (Hence, "The Human Windmill.") Greb, who died young, was a world middleweight champion for three years but a flamboyant presence in boxing circles for a long time. After the first of his several fights with Greb the twenty-two-year-old Tunney was so badly hurt he had to spend a week in bed; he'd lost an astonishing two quarts of blood during the fifteen-round fight. Yet, as Tunney said some years later:

> Greb gave me a terrible whipping. He broke my nose, maybe with a butt. He cut my eyes and ears, perhaps with his laces . . . My jaw was swollen from the right temple down the cheek, along under the chin and partway up the other side. The referee, the ring itself, was full of blood . . . But it was in that first fight, in which I lost my American light-heavyweight title, that I knew I had found a way to beat Harry eventually. I was fortunate, really. If boxing in those days had been afflicted with the Commission doctors we have today—

who are always poking their noses into the ring and examining superficial wounds—the first fight with Greb would have been stopped before I learned how to beat him. It's possible, even probable, that if this had happened I would never have been heard of again.

Tunney's career, in other words, was built upon pain. Without it he would never have moved up into Dempsey's class.

Tommy Loughran, light-heavyweight champion in the years 1927–29, was a master boxer greatly admired by other boxers. He approached boxing literally as a science—as Tunney did—studying his opponents' styles and mapping out ring strategy for each fight, as boxers and their trainers commonly do today. Loughran rigged up mirrors in his basement so that he could watch himself as he worked out, for, as he said, no boxer ever sees himself quite as he appears to his opponent. He sees the opponent but not himself as an opponent. The secret of Loughran's career was that his right hand broke easily so that he was forced to use it only once each fight: for the knockout punch or nothing. "I'd get one shot then the agony of the thing would hurt me if the guy got up," Loughran said. "Anybody I ever hit with a left hook I knocked flat on his face, but I would never take a chance for fear if my [left hand] goes, I'm done for."

Both Tunney and Loughran, it is instructive to note, retired from boxing well before they were forced to retire. Tunney became a highly successful businessman, and

Loughran a highly successful sugar broker on the Wall Street commodities market. (Just to suggest that boxers are not invariably stupid, illiterate, or punch-drunk.)

Then there was Carmen Basilio!—much loved for his audacious ring style, his hit-and-be-hit approach. Basilio was world middle- and welterweight champion 1953–57, stoic, determined, a slugger willing to get hit in order to deal powerful counter-punches of his own. Onlookers marveled at the punishment Basilio seemed to absorb though Basilio insisted that he didn't get hit the way people believed. And when he was hit, and hit hard—

> People don't realize how you're affected by a knockout punch when you're hit on the chin. It's nerves is all it is. There's no real concussion as far as the brain is concerned. I got hit on the point of the chin [in a match with Tony DeMarco in 1955]. It was a left hook that hit the right point of my chin. What happens is it pulls your jawbone out of your socket from the right side and jams it into the left side and the nerve there paralyzed the whole left side of my body, especially my legs. My left knee buckled and I almost went down, but when I got back to my corner the bottom of my foot felt like it had needles about six inches high and I just kept stamping my foot on the floor, trying to bring it back. And by the time the bell rang it was all right.

Basilio belongs to the rough-and-tumble era of LaMotta, Graziano, Zale, Pep, Saddler; Gene Fullmer, Dick Tiger, Kid Gavilan. An era when, if two boxers wanted to fight dirty, the referee was likely to give them license, or at least not to interfere.

Of Muhammad Ali in his prime Norman Mailer observed, "He worked apparently on the premise that there was something obscene about being hit." But in fights in his later career, as with George Foreman in Zaire, even Muhammad Ali was willing to be hit, and to be hurt, in order to wear down an opponent. Brawling fighters—those with "heart" like Jake LaMotta, Rocky Graziano, Ray Mancini—have little choice but to absorb terrible punishment in exchange for some advantage (which does not in any case always come). And surely it is true that some boxers (see Jake LaMotta's autobiographical *Raging Bull*) invite injury as a means of assuaging guilt, in a Dostoyevskian exchange of physical well-being for peace of mind. Boxing is about being hit rather more than it is about hitting, just as it is about feeling pain, if not devastating psychological paralysis, more than it is about winning. One sees clearly from the "tragic" careers of any number of boxers that the boxer prefers physical pain in the ring to the absence of pain that is ideally the condition of ordinary life. If one cannot hit, one can yet be hit, and know that one is still alive.

It might be said that boxing is primarily about maintaining a body capable of entering combat against other well-conditioned bodies. Not the public spectacle, the fight itself, but the rigorous training period leading up to it demands the most discipline, and is believed to be the chief cause of the boxer's physical and mental infirmities. (As a boxer ages his sparring partners get younger, the game itself gets more desperate.)

The artist senses some kinship, however oblique and one-sided, with the professional boxer in this matter of training. This fanatic subordination of the self in terms of a wished-for destiny. One might compare the time-bound public spectacle of the boxing match (which could be as brief as an ignominious forty-five seconds—the record for a title fight!) with the publication of a writer's book. That which is "public" is but the final stage in a protracted, arduous, grueling, and frequently despairing period of preparation. Indeed, one of the reasons for the habitual attraction of serious writers to boxing (from Swift, Pope, Johnson to Hazlitt, Lord Byron, Hemingway, and our own Norman Mailer, George Plimpton, Ted Hoagland, Wilfrid Sheed, Daniel Halpern, et al.) is the sport's systematic cultivation of pain in the interests of a project, a life-goal: the willed transposing of the sensation we know as pain (physical, psychological, emotional) into its polar opposite. If this is masochism—and I doubt that it is, or that it is simply—it is also intelligence, cunning, strategy. It is an act of consummate self-determination—the constant re-establishment of the parameters of one's being. To not only accept but to actively invite what most sane creatures avoid—pain, humiliation, loss, chaos—is to experience the present moment as already, in a sense, past. *Here* and *now* are but part of the design of *there* and *then:* pain now but control, and therefore triumph, later. And pain itself is miraculously transposed by that of its contest. Indeed, it might be said that "contest" is all.

necessary. It is important to get your mind off the fight.

Of all boxers it seems to have been Rocky Marciano (still our only undefeated heavyweight champion) who trained with the most monastic devotion; his training methods have become legendary. In contrast to reckless fighters like Harry "The Human Windmill" Greb, who kept in

but control, and therefore triumph, later. And pain itself
is miraculously transposed by dint of its context. Indeed,
it might be said that "context" is all.

The novelist George Garrett, an amateur boxer of
some decades ago, reminisces about his training period:

> I learned something . . . about the brotherhood of
> boxers. People went into this brutal and often self-de-
> structive activity for a rich variety of motivations, most
> of them bitterly antisocial and verging on the psy-
> chotic. Most of the fighters I knew of were wounded
> people who felt a deep, powerful urge to wound others at
> real risk to themselves. In the beginning. What hap-
> pened was that in almost every case, there was so much
> self-discipline required and craft involved, so much else
> besides one's original motivations to concentrate on,
> that these motivations became at least cloudy and
> vague and were often forgotten, lost completely. Many
> good and experienced fighters (as has often been noted)
> become gentle and kind people . . . They have the
> habit of leaving all their fight in the ring. And even
> there, in the ring, it is dangerous to invoke too much
> anger. It can be a stimulant, but is very expensive of
> energy. It is impractical to get mad most of the time.

Of all boxers it seems to have been Rocky Marciano (still
our only undefeated heavyweight champion) who trained
with the most monastic devotion; his training methods
have become legendary. In contrast to reckless fighters
like Harry "The Human Windmill" Greb, who kept in

condition by boxing all the time, Marciano was willing to seclude himself from the world, including his wife and family, for as long as three months before a fight. Apart from the grueling physical ordeal of this period and the obsessive preoccupation with diet and weight and muscle tone, Marciano concentrated on one thing: the upcoming fight. Every minute of his life was defined in terms of the opening second of the fight. In his training camp the opponent's name was never mentioned in Marciano's hearing, nor was boxing as a subject discussed. In the final month Marciano would not write a letter since a letter related to the outside world. During the last ten days before a fight he would see no mail, take no telephone calls, meet no new acquaintances. During the week before the fight he would not shake hands. Or go for a ride in a car, however brief. No new foods! No dreaming of the morning after the fight! For all that was not *the fight* had to be excluded from consciousness. When Marciano worked out with a punching bag he saw his opponent before him, when he jogged he saw his opponent close beside him, no doubt when he slept he "saw" his opponent constantly— as the cloistered monk or nun chooses by an act of fanatical will to "see" only God.

Madness?—or merely discipline?—this absolute subordination of the self. In any case, for Marciano, it worked.

*Tommy Hearns was a little cocky,
and I had something for him.*
—*MARVIN HAGLER*

No sport is more physical, more direct, than boxing. No sport appears more powerfully homoerotic: the confrontation in the ring—the disrobing—the sweaty heated combat that is part dance, courtship, coupling—the frequent urgent pursuit by one boxer of the other in the fight's natural and violent movement toward the "knockout": surely boxing derives much of its appeal from this mimicry of a species of erotic love in which one man overcomes the other in an exhibition of superior strength and will. The heralded celibacy of the fighter-in-training is very much a part of boxing lore: instead of focusing his energies and fantasies upon a woman the boxer focuses them upon an opponent. Where Woman has been, Opponent must be.

As Ali's Bundini Brown has said: "You got to get the hard-on, and then you got to keep it. You want to be careful not to lose the hard-on, and cautious not to come."

Most fights, however fought, end with an embrace

between the boxers after the final bell—a gesture of mutual respect and apparent affection that appears to the onlooker to be more than perfunctory. Rocky Graziano sometimes kissed his opponents out of gratitude for the fight. One might wonder if the boxing match leads irresistibly to this moment: the public embrace of two men who otherwise, in public or in private, could never approach each other with such passion. Though many men are loudly contemptuous of weakness (as if eager to dissociate themselves from it: as during a boxing match when one or both boxers are unwilling to fight) a woman is struck by the admiration, amounting at times to awe, they will express for a man who has exhibited superior courage while losing his fight. And they will express tenderness for injured boxers, even if it is only by way of commentary on photographs: the picture of Ray Mancini after his second defeat by Livingstone Bramble, for instance, when Mancini's face was hideously battered (photographs in *Sports Illustrated* and elsewhere were gory, near-pornographic); the much-reprinted photograph of the defeated Thomas Hearns being carried to his corner in the arms of an enormous black man (a bodyguard, one assumes) in solemn formal attire—Hearns the "Hit Man" now helpless, semiconscious, looking very like a black Christ taken from the cross. These are powerful, haunting, unsettling images, cruelly beautiful, inextricably bound up with boxing's primordial appeal.

Yet to suggest that men might love and respect one another directly, without the violent ritual of combat, is to misread man's greatest passion—for war, not peace. Love, if there is to be love, comes second.

I know I'm not a bad fighter. I try so hard at something I like doing. I love boxing. I dream of being a fighter. I see myself winning the title. I don't know which one. I see myself being picked up, carried around, getting my belt. Sometimes I see it in slow motion . . .

—a thirty-four-year-old welterweight who has lost nearly all his fights, usually by knockouts

A n "opponent" is known in the boxing trade as a man who loses, and is dependable. Matched with a younger, promising boxer with financial backing he will give a decent showing, he will very likely not collapse in the opening seconds of the opening round, and he will not, certainly, mar the record of the other boxer. He may have dreams of winning a "title" but his value to the trade is that he helps to build up (i.e., to inflate) another boxer's record. His name is always unknown—indeed, he is likely

to have several names or aliases. His career is a foregone
conclusion: he has none. He works for a living by way of
being a human punching bag.

Opponents are also known as "stiffs" and "bums"—
as in Joe Louis's "Bum-of-the-Month" matches after Louis
had cleared the heavyweight division of serious contenders for his title.

The world's consistently highest-paid athletes are
American boxers but it does not follow that boxers as a
class are the highest paid athletes. The very opposite is
the case. Impoverished people prostitute themselves in
ways available to them, and boxing on its lowest levels
offers an opportunity for men to make a living of a kind.
In fact, if a boxer is fortunate and isn't injured, boxing
will pay him better wages than most of the jobs available
to unskilled and uneducated men in our post-industrial
society. (After Michael Spinks won an Olympic gold
medal he quit boxing and went to work scrubbing floors
and cleaning toilets in a St. Louis chemical factory. But
conditions in the factory were so bad he had to return, he
said, to boxing: "Heck, breathing those chemicals, I could
have died faster there than in the ring.") And boxing in
circumstances where casino gambling and not safety is a
priority—Atlantic City, for instance, and not New York
City with its stringent boxing regulations—is likely to be
highly tempting. The top of the pyramid is small, the base
broad, shading out into the anonymous subsoil of humanity.

The Ring magazine, "The Bible of Boxing," pub-

lishes the results of over one thousand fights in every
issue. Even boxing's many ranked and overrated boxers
constitute a small number of the men who are licensed to
box in the United States and elsewhere. *The Ring Record
Book* lists such boxers as Johnny D. (who has lost sixteen
fights in a row, twelve by knockouts); Marcus D. (who won
only his first fight years ago and has lost each subsequent
match); Obie G. (who has had nine fights and has been
knocked out nine times); Irving B. (who has had seven
fights and has been knocked out seven times, always in
the first or second round). It is such professional opponents who account for the unblemished records of others
—for clearly, the up-and-coming with their straight wins
and zero losses cannot have been fighting one another.

(During the 1920s when boxing was officially banned
in New York, boxers fought in private clubs, not unlike
speakeasies, in wholly unsupervised circumstances. Budd
Schulberg writes that during the years boxing was outlawed there were in fact many more matches in New York
City than there are now: each borough had its own clubs,
matches were held every night of the week, boxers of all
weights, ages, experience, and abilities were thrown hap-
hazardly together, and, if a match resulted in death, the
boxer's body was likely to be dumped without identification in the river.)

With the complicity of managers and promoters, boxers of this class frequently fight under several aliases, and
even with present-day regulations (in New York and Pennsylvania, for instance, a fighter who has been knocked out

is automatically suspended for ninety days; in New Jersey, for sixty days) it is extremely difficult to prevent them from doing themselves harm. Desperation for money or simply for "fame" cannot be regulated. Identification is made not with boxing's limitless supply of losers but with boxing's very few stars, as in any other profession in which the individual can be, by way of his own intransigent will, glorified. As a trainer of opponents says, perhaps not even cynically: "There's a new guy walking in the gym every day."

*When you're fighting you're fighting
for one thing: money.*
—JACK DEMPSEY,
former heavyweight champion of the world

That boxing is our most controversial sport, always, it seems, on the very threshold of oblivion, has not prevented it from having become a multimillion-dollar business.

For the past several years the three highest-paid athletes in the world have been American boxers. (In 1985 Larry Holmes reported an income of a little more than

$6.5 million; Marvin Hagler, a little more than $5 million; Thomas Hearns, approximately $5 million. By contrast, the fourth highest-paid athlete, a celebrated football player, reported an income of only—only!—$3 million.) In his long and spotty career Jack Dempsey earned $3,500,000—prodigious for his time, though the equivalent today of only $28 million. Muhammad Ali, who earned somewhere beyond $70 million through his long career, is generally believed to be the most highly paid athlete in world history; his successor Larry Holmes is believed to have earned nearly that much. (Though figures vary, and Holmes's career, at the time of this writing, is still extant; he claims to have $99 million in the bank—with more to come.) Individual boxing matches sometimes bring in extraordinary sums for boxers, even accounting for the money drawn off by promoters: the losing challenger Thomas Hearns made at least $7 million in his eight-minute fight with Marvin Hagler, while Hagler made at least $7.5 million; for the first of his highly publicized matches with Roberto Durán in 1980—which he lost on points—the popular welterweight champion Sugar Ray Leonard was paid $10 million (to Durán's $2 million). One of the focal arguments for a title fight between Marvin Hagler and Sugar Ray Leonard was that the gate would very likely be the highest in all of boxing history: a promoter's dream. And none of these figures takes into account various subsidiary earnings from television appearances and commercials which, in Leonard's case, have certainly been substantial.

Indeed, these subsidiary earnings have become, for many boxers, the measure of their worth beyond the ring: the assessment, in dollars, of "consumer acceptance" of their images. *(The Ring* magazine is beginning to note the sums earned by boxers giving television endorsements of products . . . a new kind of ring "record," it might be said.)

Money has drawn any number of retired boxers back into the ring, frequently with tragic results. The most notorious example still remains Joe Louis, who, in a desperate attempt to pay money owed in back taxes, continued fighting well beyond the point at which he could defend himself against younger heavyweights. After a career of seventeen years during which Louis virtually came to typify boxing internationally he was finally—and ignominiously—stopped by the much younger Rocky Marciano (who was as grieved by his victory as Louis by the defeat). Louis then took on a degrading second career as a professional wrestler, which ended abruptly in 1956 when, aged forty-two, he suffered injuries to his heart muscles after three-hundred-pound "Rocky Lee" stepped on his chest.

Ezzard Charles, Jersey Joe Walcott, Joe Frazier, Muhammad Ali, most recently Larry Holmes—each heavyweight champion or ex-champion continued fighting well beyond the point at which he could safely defend himself. If Ali had retired permanently at the age of thirty-six—if he had not, contrary to his physician's advice, insisted upon fighting, two years later, the much-younger Larry Holmes—perhaps his story would have a happier ending. (When Ali was told in the mid-1970s to retire by his personal physician Ferdie Pacheco his response was to fire Pacheco.) Of all heavyweight champions only Rocky Marciano, to whom fame and money were evidently not of paramount importance, was wise enough to retire before he was defeated.

In any case, a boxer's passion for money—for the prodigious sums earned by a very few champions—does not account for the fact that a public is willing, if not eager, to pay them these sums. Private and public obsessions mimic one another but are not identical.

> *Boxing is the sport to which*
> *all other sports aspire.*
> —*GEORGE FOREMAN,*
> former heavyweight champion of the world

At least in theory and by way of tradition boxing is a sport. But what *is* sport?—and why is a man, *in* sport, not the man he is or is expected to be at other times?

Consider the history of gladiatorial combat as the Romans practiced it, or caused it to be practiced, from approximately 265 B.C. to its abolishment by Theodoric in A.D. 500. In the ancient world, among part-civilized nations, it was customary after a battle to sacrifice prisoners of war in honor of commanders who had been killed. It also became customary to sacrifice slaves at the funerals of all persons of importance. But then—for what reason?— for amusement, or for the sake of "sport"?—the condemned slaves were given arms and urged to defend themselves by killing the men who were ordered to kill them. Out of this evolution of brute sacrifice into something approaching a recognizable sporting contest the notorious phenomenon of Roman gladitorial combat—death as mass amusement—gradually arose. Surely there is nothing quite like it in world history.

At first the contests were performed at the funeral pyre or near the sepulcher, but, with the passage of time, as interest in the fighting detached itself from its ostensibly religious context, matches were moved to the Forum, then to the Circus and amphitheaters. Contractors emerged to train the slaves, men of rank and political importance began to keep "families" of gladiators, upcoming fights were promoted and advertised as sporting contests are today, shows lasting as long as three days increased in number and popularity. Not the mere sacrifice of helpless individuals but the "sport" of the contest excited spectators, for, though the instinct to fight and to kill is surely qualified by one's personal courage, the instinct to watch others fight and kill is evidently inborn. When the boxing fan shouts, "Kill him! Kill him!" he is betraying no peculiar individual pathology or quirk but asserting his common humanity and his kinship, however distant, with the thousands upon thousands of spectators who crowded into the Roman amphitheaters to see gladiators fight to the death. That such contests for mass amusement endured not for a few years or even decades but for centuries should arrest our attention.

According to Petronius the gladiators took the following oath: "We swear, after the dictation of Eumolpus, to suffer death by fire, bonds, stripes, and the sword; and whatever else Eumolpus may command, as true gladiators we bind ourselves body and mind to our master's service." Their courage became legendary. Cicero referred to it as a model for all Roman citizens—that one should be willing to suffer nobly in the defense of the Commonwealth. In general, gladiators were slaves and condemned criminals who could hope to prolong their lives or even, if they were champions, to gain freedom; but impoverished freemen often fought as well. With the passage of time, paralleling and surely contributing to what we see as the decadence of Rome, even men of rank volunteered to compete publicly. (Under Nero, that most notorious of Roman emperors, such wild exhibitions flourished. It is estimated that during his reign from A.D. 54 to 68 as many as one thousand aristocrats performed as gladiators in one way or another, in fights fair, handicapped, or fixed. At times even women of rank competed—which matches were no doubt particularly noteworthy.) So drawn to these violent sports were Roman aristocrats that the Emperor Augustus was finally moved to issue an edict forbidding them to train as gladiators.

The origins of gladiatorial boxing are specifically Greek. According to tradition a ruler named Thesus (circa 900 B.C.) was entertained by the spectacle of two matched fighters, seated, facing each other, hammering each other to death with their fists. Eventually the men fought on their feet and covered their fists with leather thongs; then with leather thongs covered with sharp metal spikes—the cestus. A ring of some kind, probably a circle, became a neutral space to which an injured boxer might temporarily retreat. When the Romans cultivated the sport it became extremely popular: one legendary cestus-champion was said to have killed 1,425 opponents. Winning gladiators were widely celebrated as "kings of athletes" and heroes for all. By confirming in the public arena the bloody mortality of other men they established for themselves, as champions always do, a kind of immortality.

So it happens that the wealthier and more advanced a society, the more fanatic its interest in certain kinds of sport. Civilization's trajectory is to curve back upon itself —naturally? helplessly?—like the mythical snake biting its own tail and to take up with passion the outward signs and gestures of "savagery." While it is plausible that emotionally effete men and women may require ever more extreme experiences to arouse them, it is perhaps the case too that the desire is not merely to *mimic* but, magically, to *be* brute, primitive, instinctive, and therefore innocent. One might then be a person for whom the contest is not mere self-destructive play but life itself; and the world, not in spectacular and irrevocable decline, but new, fresh, vital, terrifying and exhilarating by turns, a place of wonders. It is the lost ancestral self that is sought, however futilely. Like those dream-remnants of childhood that year by year continue to elude us but are never abandoned, still less despised, for that reason.

Roman gladiatorial combat was abolished under the Christian emperors Constantine and Theodoric, and its practice discontinued forever. Boxing as we know it in the United States derives solely from English bare-knuckle prizefighting of the eighteenth century and from an entirely different conception of sport.

The first recorded account of a bare-knuckle fight in England—between "a gentleman's footman and a butcher"—is dated 1681 and appeared in a publication called the *London Protestant Mercury*. This species of fight, in which maiming and death were not the point, was known as a "Prize Fight" or the "Prize Ring," and was public entertainment of an itinerant nature, frequently attached to village fairs. The Prize Ring was a movable space created by spectators who formed a loose circle by holding a length of rope; the Prize Fight was a voluntary contest between two men, usually a "champion" and a "challenger," unrefereed but governed by rudimentary rules of fair play. The challenge to fight was put to a

crowd by a fighter and his accomplices and if any man
wanted to accept he tossed his hat into the ring—hence
the political expression with its overtone of bellicosity—
and the fight was on. Bets were commonly placed on
which man would knock the other down first or draw
"first blood." Foul play was actively discouraged by the
crowd; the fighters shook hands after the fight. "The Noble Art," as prizefighting was called, began as a low-life
species of entertainment but was in time enthusiastically
supported by sporting members of the aristocracy and the
upper classes.

England's earliest bare-knuckle champion was a man
named James Figg who won the honor in 1719. The last
of the bare-knuckle champions was the American heavyweight John L. Sullivan whose career—from approximately 1882 to 1892—overlapped both bare-knuckle
fighting and gloved boxing as established under the rules
of the Marquis of Queensberry which are observed, with
some elaboration, to the present time. The most significant changes were two: the introduction of leather gloves
(mainly to protect the hand, not the face—a man's knuck-
les are easily broken) and the third man in the ring, the
referee, whose privilege it is to stop the fight at his own
discretion, if he thinks a boxer has no chance of winning
or cannot defend himself against his opponent. With the
introduction of the referee the crudeness of "The Noble
Art" passes over into the relative sophistication of boxing.

The "third man in the ring," usually anonymous so far as the crowd is concerned, appears to many observers no more than an observer himself, even an intruder; a ghostly presence as fluid in motion and quick-footed as the boxers themselves (indeed, he is frequently an ex-boxer). But so central to the drama of boxing is the referee that the spectacle of two men fighting each other unsupervised in an elevated ring would seem hellish, if not obscene—life rather than art. The referee makes boxing possible.

The referee is our intermediary in the fight. He is our moral conscience extracted from us as spectators so that, for the duration of the fight, "conscience" need not be a factor in our experience; nor need it be a factor in the boxers' behavior. (Asked if boxers are ever sorry for having hurt their opponents, Carmen Basilio replied: "Sorry? Are you kidding? Boxers are never sorry.") Which is not to say that boxers are always and forever without conscience: all boxers are different, and behave differently at different times. But there are occasions when a boxer who is trapped in the ropes and unable to fall to the canvas while being struck repeatedly is in danger of being killed unless the referee intervenes—the attacking boxer has been trained not to stop his attack while his opponent is still technically standing. In the rapidly escalating intensity of the fight only the referee remains neutral and objective.

Though the referee's role is highly demanding and it has been estimated that there are perhaps no more than a dozen really skilled referees in the world, it seems necessary in the drama of the fight that the referee himself possesses no dramatic identity: referees' names are rarely remembered after a fight except by seasoned boxing fans. Yet, paradoxically, the referee's participation is crucial. He cannot control what happens in the ring but he can control to a degree *that* it happens—he is responsible for the fight if not for the individual fighters' performances. In a match in which boxing skills and not merely fighting are predominant the referee's role can be merely functional, but in a fiercely contested match it is of incalculable importance. The referee holds the power of life and death at certain times since his decision to terminate a fight, or to allow it to continue, can determine a boxer's fate. (One should know that a well-aimed punch with a heavyweight's full weight behind it can have the equivalent force of ten thousand pounds—a blow that must be absorbed by the brain in its jelly sac.) In the infamous Benny Paret–Emile Griffith fight of March 1962 the referee Ruby Goldstein was said to have stood paralyzed as Griffith trapped Paret in the ropes, striking him as many as eighteen times in the head. (Paret died ten days later.) Boxers are trained not to quit. If knocked down, they try to get up to continue the fight, even if they can hardly defend themselves. The primary rule of the ring—to defend oneself at all times—is both a parody and a distillation of life.

In the past—well into the 1950s—it was not customary for a referee to interfere with a fight, however brutal and one-sided. A boxer who kept struggling to his feet after having been knocked down, or, like the intransigent Jake LaMotta in his sixth and final fight with Sugar Ray Robinson in 1951, refused to fall to the canvas though he could no longer defend himself and had become a human punching bag, was simply left to his fate. The will of the crowd—and overwhelmingly it *is* the will of the crowd—that one man defeat the other totally and irrevocably, was honored. Hence the bloody "great" fights of boxing's history—Dempsey's triumph over Willard, for instance—inconceivable today.

It should be understood that "boxing" and "fighting," though always combined in the greatest of boxers, can be entirely different and even unrelated activities. Amateur boxers are trained to win their matches on points; professionals usually try for knockouts. (Not that professionals are more violent than amateurs but why trust judges?—and the knockout is dramatically spectacular.) If boxing is frequently, in the lighter weights especially, a highly complex and refined skill, belonging solely to civilization, fighting belongs to something predating civilization, the instinct not merely to defend oneself—for how has the masculine ego ever been assuaged by so minimal a response to threat?—but to attack another and to force him into absolute submission. This accounts for the electrifying effect upon a typical fight crowd when fighting suddenly emerges out of boxing—when, for instance, a boxer's face begins to bleed and the fight seems to enter a new and more dangerous phase. The flash of red is the visible sign of the fight's authenticity in the eyes of many spectators and boxers are justified in being proud, as many are, of their facial scars.

If the "violence" of boxing seems at times to flow from the crowd, to be a heightened expression of the crowd's delirium—rarely transmitted by television, by the way—the many restraints and subtleties of boxing are possible because of the "third man in the ring," a counter of sorts to the inchoate wash of emotion beyond the ropes and the ring apron: our conscience, as I've indicated, extracted from us, and granted an absolute authority.

. . . Whether [this] makes me a humanist or a voyeur, I'm not sure.
—JOHN SCHULIAN,
sportswriter

Writers have long been attracted to boxing, from the early days of the English Prize Ring to the present time. Its most immediate appeal is that of the spectacle, in itself wordless, lacking a language, that requires others to define it, celebrate it, complete it. Like all extreme but perishable human actions boxing excites not

only the writer's imagination, but also his instinct to bear witness. Before film and tape, this instinct must have been particularly acute. (Consider a sport that often took place illegally, many of its most famous fights fought on barges, on islands, in outlaw territory between states, involving the risk of arrest for both performers and observers: what passion!) And boxers have frequently displayed themselves, inside the ring and out, as characters in the literary sense of the word. *Extravagant fictions without a structure to contain them.*

In the days of the Prize Ring, accounts of fights were often in verse, accompanied by cartoon-like drawings, printed on broadsides, and sold by itinerant salesmen. From approximately 1700 onward—according to boxing historian Pierce Egan—most English newspapers, including the fashionable *The Times*, carried detailed accounts of fights; and in 1818 Egan brought out the first edition of his famous *Boxiana: Sketches of Ancient and Modern Pugilism*, which covered the Prize Ring from its earliest days to Egan's own when, though wildly popular, Prize Fighting was officially illegal and announcements of impending matches were by way of rumor. (Any number of editions of *Boxiana* have been printed, the most recent being in the 1970s.) Egan's zest for his outlaw subject is communicated in prose of a particularly vigorous kind—colorful, direct, blunt, "masculine," yet as subtly and as wittily nuanced as that of his eighteenth-century predecessors Defoe, Swift, Pope, Fielding, Churchill. It is Egan who called fighting "the Sweet Science of Bruising" and it is

Egan whom A. J. Liebling most frequently cites and acknowledges as his master in *The Sweet Science*, a *boxiana*
of modern times much admired by boxing enthusiasts.

(I sense myself uneasily alone in disliking much of
Liebling, for his relentlessly jokey, condescending, and
occasionally racist attitude toward his subject. Perhaps
because it was originally published in *The New Yorker* in
the early 1950s *The Sweet Science: Boxing and Boxiana—a
Ringside View* is a peculiarly self-conscious assemblage of
pieces, arch, broad in its humor, rather like situation comedy in which boxers are "characters" depicted for our
amusement. Liebling is uncertain even about such champions as Louis, Marciano, and Robinson—should one re-
vere, or mock? And he is pitiless when writing about
"Hurricane" Jackson, a black boxer cruelly called an animal, an "it," because of his poor boxing skills and what
Liebling considers his mental inferiority. The problem for
Liebling and for *The New Yorker* must have been how to
sell a blood sport like boxing to a genteel, affluent reader-
ship to whom the idea of men fighting for their lives
would have been deeply offensive; how to suggest boxing's
drama while skirting boxing's tragedy. It is a problem
that, for all his verbal cleverness, Liebling never entirely
solves.)

A good deal has been made of Ernest Hemingway's
attraction to boxing yet Hemingway never wrote about
boxing with the sympathy or perception with which he
wrote about bullfighting; "Fifty Grand" and "The Bat-
tler" are not among Hemingway's best short stories, and

his portrait of the "Princeton middleweight" Robert Cohn in *The Sun Also Rises* is a startlingly crude piece of Jew-baiting, in which Cohn's boxing skills are irrelevant. (When, provoked beyond endurance, Cohn knocks down Jake Barnes and his drunken friend, the scene passes by so swiftly it makes virtually no impression on the reader.)

Far more canny and knowledgeable is Norman Mailer, whose essays on Cassius Clay/Muhammad Ali and his coevals, and on the "aesthetics of the arena" gener-ally, are as good as anything ever written on the subject. Mailer's strength lies in his recognition that the boxers are *other*—though he does not say so, even in the long extravagant meditation of *The Fight* (its title in homage to Hazlitt's great essay), it seems clear to this reader at least that Mailer cannot establish a connection between himself and the boxers: he tries heroically but he cannot under-stand them and so he is forever excluded from what, un-thinkingly, they represent: an ideal (because unthinking, unforced) masculinity, beyond all question. It is this rec-ognition of his exclusion—an exclusion very nearly as complete as, say, the exclusion of a woman from boxing's codified world—that allows for the force of Mailer's vi-sion. And since the great champions of our time have been black, Mailer's preoccupation with masculinity is a preoccupation with blackness as well. Hence these charac-teristic flights of metaphysical fancy that strike the ear with the poignancy of a lovesick lament:

*If [the heavyweights] become champions they begin to
have inner lives like Hemingway or Dostoyevsky, Tol-
stoy or Faulkner, Joyce or Melville or Conrad or Lawrence or Proust . . . Dempsey was alone and Tunney
could never explain himself and Sharkey could never
believe himself nor Schmeling nor Braddock, and Carnera was sad and Baer an indecipherable clown; great
heavyweights like Louis had the loneliness of the ages
in their silence, and men like Marciano were mystified
by a power which seemed to have been granted them.
With the advent, however, of the great modern Black
heavyweights, Patterson, Liston, then Clay and Frazier,
perhaps the loneliness gave way to what it had been
protecting itself against—a surrealistic situation unsta-
ble beyond belief. Being a Black heavyweight champion in the second half of the twentieth century (with
Black revolutions opening all over the world) was now
not unlike being Jack Johnson, Malcolm X and Frank
Costello all in one . . .*

(EXISTENTIAL ERRANDS, *"King of the Hill"*)

It cannot be a coincidence that everyone's favorite boxing
novel, Leonard Gardner's *Fat City*, is a novel less about
boxing than about the strategies of self-deception; a hand-
book of sorts in failure, in which boxing functions as the
natural activity of men totally unequipped to comprehend
life. The boxers of Gardner's Stockton, California—that
notorious fight town—seem to exist in a world claustrophobic as a training gym, with no more awareness of the

great boxers of their time (would not Cassius Clay himself have been their contemporary?) than of politics and "society" in general. *Fat City* is the underside of the American dream, in which men with some minimal skill in a dangerous sport are hired to fight one another for pitifully small purses: it is a measure of the novel's irony that victory, for such stakes, is hardly to be distinguished from failure. Leonard Gardner seems to have written no other fiction, but his several articles on boxing—published in such magazines as *Sports Illustrated* and *Esquire*—display a remarkable gift for realizing, as if from the inside, the psychology of the man born to fight, the man who knows nothing *but* fighting, no matter the suicidal nature of his calling.

W. C. Heinz and Ted Hoagland have written highly regarded novels about boxing, *The Professional* and *The Circle Home* respectively, though Hoagland's novel is something of an anomaly: there are no fights in it, only training scenes, rendered with a mesmerizing kinetic precision. Budd Schulberg, Irwin Shaw, Nelson Algren, Ring Lardner, James Farrell, John O'Hara, Jack London—all have written stories about boxers, of varying worth and seriousness.

What might be called the romance of boxing—and even the sordid, filmed, *is* romance—underlies a number of Hollywood movies of similarly uneven worth, the most extraordinary being Martin Scorsese's award-winning *Raging Bull*, in which Robert De Niro almost literally transforms himself into Jake LaMotta. Other notable films

in this genre are *Fat City, Champion, Somebody Up There Likes Me* (based on the Rocky Graziano autobiography), *The Harder They Fall, The Set-Up, The Champ, Body and Soul, Requiem for a Heavyweight,* and *The Great White Hope*—the last two based on successful plays. And then there are the "Rocky" movies, scarcely about boxing as we know it (Rocky and his heavyweight opponents are, for one thing, ludicrously encumbered with bodybuilders' physiques, not boxers') but effective as pop-iconographic success stories starring Sylvester Stallone as Rocky, "The Italian Stallion," the sweet tough guy, the perpetual underdog who cannot lose even against overwhelming odds. Rocky is a comic book boxer, his matches are comic book matches, like the exploits of his look-alike Rambo, who embodies even more powerfully than Rocky America's fascination with the (male) *isolato* whose orientation to the world is purely physical. Yet it is significant, certainly, that Stallone made Rocky a boxer, in homage to heavyweight champion Rocky Marciano, whose ring style he imitates—to a degree.

Boxing has often stimulated first-rate sportswriting, that most taxing of genres. Among contemporary sportswriters John Schulian (of the Philadelphia *Daily News)* and Hugh McIlvanney (of the English *The Observer)* are outstanding for the consistently high quality of their prose and for what might be called their rigorously analytical approach to their subject: not merely *what,* and *how,* but in fact *why*—why does boxing exist, why are men (and some women) fascinated by it, what does it tell us about the human predicament? Schulian's *Writers' Fighters* and McIlvanney's *McIlvanney on Boxing* bring together columns published over a period of time but are notable for the unity of their respective visions. Neither writer takes his subject for granted, nor does he draw back from examining the ambivalent relationship between the man who writes about boxing and boxing itself, "the sweet science of bruising." Other sports draw forth other responses, but boxing is, here as elsewhere, a special case. In no other sport is the connection between performer and observer so intimate, so frequently painful, so unresolved.

That no other sport can elicit such *theoretical* anxiety lies at the heart of boxing's fascination for the writer. It is the thing in itself but it is also its meaning to the individual, shifting and problematic as a blurred image in a mirror. The writer contemplates his opposite in the boxer, who is all public display, all risk and, ideally, improvisation: he will know his limit in a way that the writer, like all artists, never quite knows his limit—for we who write live in a kaleidoscopic world of ever-shifting assessments and judgments, unable to determine whether it is revelation or supreme self-delusion that fuels our most crucial efforts. Setting aside for a moment the problem of incompetent or biased judges, of the kind that gave Michael Spinks a victory over Larry Holmes in Spinks's title defense of April 1986, or had Ray Mancini outpointing Livingstone Bramble in the first of their two matches, the boxer's world is not an ambiguous one: he quickly comes to know his worth in a context of other boxers. Indeed, it is impossible not to know it. "Promising" careers are ended in a matter of seconds; "comebacks" are revealed as mere mistakes; a young and unranked contender (like "Lightning" Lonnie Smith in his title match against junior welterweight champion Billy Costello) leaps immediately to the top. There can be no ambiguity about Marvin Hagler's defeat of John Mugabi, or Thomas Hearns's defeat of James Shuler, or the unexpected loss of his bantamweight title by Richie Sandoval to Gaby Canizales—the near loss, it seemed to some observers, of Sandoval's very life. This sense of an ending, a limit, a final and incontestable judgment—boxing in its greatest moments suggests the bloody fifth acts of classic tragedies, in which that mysterious element we call "plot" achieves closure.

For some writers the fascination has to do, as I've suggested earlier, with boxing's dazzlingly explicit display of masochism—"masochism" in its loosest, most suggestive, one might say poetic sense. For, contrary to stereotyped notions, boxing is primarily about being, and not giving, hurt. (Which the most distinguished boxing movies—*Raging Bull, Fat City, Champion*—suggest most graphically.) To move through pain to triumph—or the semblance of triumph—is the writer's, as it is the boxer's, hope. The moment of visceral horror in a typical fight, at least as I experience it, is that moment when one boxer loses control, cannot maintain his defense, begins to waver, falter, fall back, rock with his opponent's punches which he can no longer absorb; the moment in which the fight is turned around, and which an entire career, an entire life, may end. It is not an isolated moment but *the* moment—mystical, universal. The defeat of one man is the triumph of the other: but we are apt to read this "triumph" as merely temporary and provisional. Only the defeat is permanent.

When I used to dream about boxing, or about abstract, inconclusive matches between dream-opponents whose faces I could not see, I thought of boxing as a knot of sorts, tightly, cruelly knotted, there to be untied. You can't, but you must, untie it. You must—but you can't. If you untie one knot you will be confronted with another and beyond that another, and another: rounds, matches, career, "life." The difference for the boxer is that loss, humiliation, shame are only part of the risk—physical injury, even death, awaits as well. One is punished for one's failure as Kafka imagined one might be punished for one's sins, the sentence etched into flesh, killing even as it pronounces judgment.

. . . *Down there in the stable a hollow square of faces in the lantern light, the white faces on three sides, the black faces on the fourth, and in the center two of [Sutpen's] wild negroes fighting, naked, fighting not as white men fight, with rules and weapons, but as negroes fight to hurt one another quick and bad.*
—*from* WILLIAM FAULKNER'S ABSALOM, ABSALOM!

Some time ago one of the southern states adopted a new method of capital punishment. Poison gas supplanted the gallows. In its earliest stages, a microphone was placed inside the sealed death chamber so that scientific observers might hear the words of the dying prisoner . . . The first victim was a young Negro. As the pellet dropped into the container, and gas curled upward, through the microphone came these words: "Save me, Joe Louis. Save me, Joe Louis. Save me, Joe Louis . . ."

— MARTIN LUTHER KING, JR.,
quoted in Chris Mead,
CHAMPION—JOE LOUIS,
BLACK MAN IN WHITE AMERICA

It's hard being black. You ever been black? I was black once—when I was poor.

— LARRY HOLMES,
former WBC heavyweight champion

O ne's first impression is that professional boxers fighting together appear to be angry with each other, since their actions mimic anger, even rage. Why else hit, and try to injure, another person? Naturally this initial impression is misleading—boxing is "work" to most boxers and emotion has little part in it, or should have little. Indeed, highly successful champions from Jack Dempsey to Larry Holmes have insisted they fought only for money. To acknowledge other motives would suggest *machismo's* vulnerability.

Yet in a deeper sense boxers *are* angry, as even a superficial knowledge of their lives indicates. And boxing is fundamentally about anger. It is in fact the only sport in which anger is accommodated, ennobled. It is the only human activity in which rage can be transposed without equivocation into art.

Some observers—among them men—believe that boxers are angry because they are men; and anger, for men, is a means of asserting dominance over other men—a tool, one might say, of the manly trade. Yet it is reasonable to assume that boxers fight one another because the legitimate objects of their anger are not accessible to them. There is no political system in which the spectacle of two men fighting each other is not a striking, if unintended, image of the political impotence of most men (and women): You fight what's nearest, what's available, what's ready to fight you. And, if you can, you do it for money.

If boxers as a class are angry one would have to be willfully naïve not to know why. For the most part they constitute the disenfranchised of our affluent society, they are the sons of impoverished ghetto neighborhoods in which anger, if not fury, is appropriate—rather more, perhaps, than Christian meekness and self-abnegation. (It

was only in prison that Sonny Liston, one of twenty-five children born to a sharecropper's family in rural Arkansas, had enough to eat.) Where there is peace, Nietzsche theorizes, the warlike man attacks himself, but what precisely is "peace"? and where, in ghetto neighborhoods of unspeakable squalor and malaise, is it to be located? Boxing may be a way of cruelly assaulting one's self but it is most immediately a way of transcending one's fate. Going to war, like Marvin Hagler, and making millions of dollars from it, is distinctly American.

The history of boxing—of fighting—in America is very much one with the history of the black man in America. It hardly needs to be said that the armed services of recent times are comprised disproportionately of black youths; this was particularly evident in the Vietnam War. Perhaps it is less well known that in the American South, before the Civil War, white slave owners commonly pitted their Negro slaves against one another in combat, and made bets on the results. To prevent the slaves' escape, or, perhaps, to make poetically graphic the circumstances of the black men's degradation, iron collars resembling dog chains were fixed about their necks and attached to chains. Often the fights were to the death. The onlookers, of course, were white; and male.

"Fighting slave collars," as they are called, are sometimes exhibited as artifacts of a specifically American/Southern history; sometimes as instruments of torture.

At the present time, when most outstanding boxers

are black, Hispanic, or Mexican, purely "Caucasian" men begin to look anemic in the ring; a white-skinned champion (the enormously popular Barry McGuigan, for instance) is something of an anomaly, and white-skinned contenders (Gerry Cooney, Matthew Hilton, Gene Hatcher, et al.) very much in demand. One of the most popular athletes in Canada is the young welterweight Shawn O'Sullivan, so alarmingly *white* a figure in the ring, in the first fight of his televised for an American audience, the viewer sensed almost at once that his more experienced black opponent, Simon Brown, would handily defeat him. The anxieties of an earlier era—that black men would prove more "manly" than white men if allowed to fight them in fair, public fights—would seem to have come true.

It is perhaps not commonly known that a Negro heavyweight championship title existed from 1902 to 1932 when many white champions (including John L. Sullivan, Jim Jeffries, Jack Dempsey) refused to fight blacks. (In 1925 Dempsey pointedly refused to meet Harry Wills —"The Black Menace"—in a title fight urged upon him by many observers.) One wonders: who were the true world's champions in those years? And of what value are historical records when they record so blatantly the prejudices of a dominant race? As recently as 1982, after decades of exemplary black boxers—from Jack Johnson to Joe Louis to Sugar Ray Robinson to Muhammad Ali— heavyweight champion Larry Holmes drew racist slurs

and insults when he defended his title against the over-rated and overpromoted White Hope challenger Gerry Cooney (whose prefight picture, and not Holmes's, ran on the cover of *Time* magazine). It is said that on the day of the match in Las Vegas President Reagan's Secret Service installed a special telephone hookup in Cooney's dressing room so that the white boxer could be immediately congratulated if he won; there was no matching telephone in the black champion's dressing room.

Much has been made of Holmes's legendary bitter-ness, as if having earned millions of dollars—and millions of dollars for others—should tidily erase the humiliations of the past. Surely this is a psychological impossibility? Lashing out against the memory of Rocky Marciano after the first of his two controversial losses to Michael Spinks, Holmes may well have been lashing out against all white champions: "—to be technical: Rocky Marciano couldn't carry my jockstrap."

Men and women with no personal or class reason for feeling anger are inclined to dismiss the emotion, if not piously condemn it, in others. Why such discontent? why such unrest? why so *strident?* Yet this world is conceived in anger—and in hatred, and in hunger—no less than it is conceived in love: that is one of the things that boxing is about. It is so simple a thing it might be overlooked.

Those whose aggression is masked, or oblique, or unsuccessful, will always condemn it in others. They are likely to think of boxing as "primitive"—as if inhabiting the flesh were not a primitive proposition, radically inappropriate to a civilization supported by and always subordinate to physical strength: missiles, nuclear warheads. The terrible silence dramatized in the boxing ring is the silence of nature before man, before language, when the physical being alone was God.

In any case, anger is an appropriate response to certain intransigent facts of life, not a motiveless malignancy as in classic tragedy but a fully motivated and socially coherent impulse. Impotence takes many forms—one of them being the reckless physical expenditure of physical potency.

What time is it?—"Macho Time"!
—HECTOR "MACHO MAN" CAMACHO,
WBC lightweight champion

I don't want to knock my opponent out.
I want to hit him, step away, and watch him hurt.
I want his heart.
—JOE FRAZIER,
former heavyweight champion of the world

A fairy-tale proposition: the heavyweight champion is the most dangerous man on earth: the most feared, the most manly. His proper mate is very likely the fairy-tale princess whom the mirrors declare the fairest woman on earth.

Boxing is a purely masculine activity and it inhabits a purely masculine world. Which is not to suggest that most men are defined by it: clearly, most men are not. And though there are female boxers—a fact that seems to surprise, alarm, amuse—women's role in the sport has always been extremely marginal. (At the time of this writing the most famous American woman boxer is the black

champion Lady Tyger Trimiar with her shaved head and theatrical tiger-striped attire.) At boxing matches women's role is limited to that of card girl and occasional National Anthem singer: stereotypical functions usually performed in stereotypically zestful feminine ways—for women have no natural place in the spectacle otherwise. The card girls in their bathing suits and spike heels, glamour girls of the 1950s, complement the boxers in their trunks and gym shoes but are not to be taken seriously: their public exhibition of themselves involves no risk and is purely decorative. Boxing is for men, and is about men, and *is* men. A celebration of the lost religion of masculinity all the more trenchant for its being lost.

In this world, strength of a certain kind—matched of course with intelligence and tirelessly developed skills—determines masculinity. Just as a boxer is his body, a man's masculinity is his use of his body. But it is also his triumph over another's use of his body. The Opponent is always male, the Opponent is the rival for one's own masculinity, most fully and combatively realized. Sugar Ray Leonard speaks of coming out of retirement to fight one man, Marvin Hagler: "I want Hagler. I need that man." Thomas Hearns, decisively beaten by Hagler, speaks of having been obsessed with him: "I want the rematch badly . . . there hasn't been a minute or an hour in any day that I haven't thought about it." Hence women's characteristic repugnance for boxing per se coupled with an intense interest in and curiosity about men's fascination with it. Men fighting men to determine worth (i.e., masculinity) excludes women as completely as the female experience of childbirth excludes men. And is there, perhaps, some connection?

In any case, raw aggression is thought to be the peculiar province of men, as nurturing is the peculiar province of women. (The female boxer violates this stereotype and cannot be taken seriously—she is parody, she is cartoon, she is monstrous. Had she an ideology, she is likely to be a feminist.) The psychologist Erik Erikson discovered that, while little girls playing with blocks generally create pleasant interior spaces and attractive entrances, little boys are inclined to pile up the blocks as high as they can and then watch them fall down: "the contemplation of ruins," Erikson observes, "is a masculine specialty." No matter the mesmerizing grace and beauty of a great boxing match, it is the catastrophic finale for which everyone waits, and hopes: the blocks piled as high as they can possibly be piled, then brought spectacularly down. Women, watching a boxing match, are likely to identify with the losing, or hurt, boxer; men are likely to identify with the winning boxer. There is a point at which male spectators are able to identify with the fight itself as, it might be said, a Platonic experience abstracted from its particulars; if they have favored one boxer over the other, and that boxer is losing, they can shift their loyalty to the winner—or, rather, "loyalty" shifts, apart from conscious volition. In that way the ritual of fighting is always honored. The high worth of combat is always affirmed.

Boxing's very vocabulary suggests a patriarchal

world taken over by adolescents. This world is young. Its focus is youth. Its focus is of course *macho—machismo* raised beyond parody. To enter the claustrophobic world of professional boxing even as a spectator is to enter what appears to be a distillation of the masculine world, empty now of women, its fantasies, hopes, and stratagems magnified as in a distorting mirror, or a dream.

Here, we find ourselves through the looking-glass. Values are reversed, evaginated: a boxer is valued not for his humanity but for being a "killer," a "mauler," a "hitman," an "animal," for being "savage," "merciless," "devastating," "ferocious," "vicious," "murderous." Opponents are not merely defeated as in a game but are "decked," "stiffed," "starched," "iced," "destroyed," "annihilated." Even the veteran sportswriters of so respectable a publication as *The Ring* are likely to be pitiless toward a boxer who has been beaten. Much of the appeal of Roberto Durán for intellectual boxing *aficionados* no less than for those whom one might suppose his natural constituency was that he seemed truly to want to kill his opponents: in his prime he was the "baby-faced assassin" with the "dead eyes" and "deadpan" expression who once said, having knocked out an opponent named Ray Lampkin, that he hadn't trained for the fight—next time he would kill the man. (According to legend Durán once felled a horse with a single blow.) Sonny Liston was another champion lauded for his menace, so different in spirit from Floyd Patterson as to seem to belong to another subspecies; to watch Liston overcome Patterson in tapes of their fights in the early 1960s is to watch the defeat of "civilization" by something so elemental and primitive it cannot be named. Masculinity in these terms is strictly hierarchical—two men cannot occupy the same space at the same time.

At the present time twenty-year-old Mike Tyson, Cus D'Amato's much-vaunted protégé, is being groomed as the most dangerous man in the heavyweight division. He is spoken of with awe as a "young bull"; his strength is prodigious, at least as demonstrated against fairly hapless, stationary opponents; he enters the arena robeless—"I feel more like a warrior"—and gleaming with sweat. He does not even wear socks. His boxing model is not Muhammad Ali, the most brilliant heavyweight of modern times, but Rocky Marciano, graceless, heavy-footed, indomitable, the man with the massive right-hand punch who was willing to absorb five blows in the hope of landing one. It was after having broken Jesse Ferguson's nose in a recent match that Tyson told reporters that it was his strategy to try to drive the bone back into the brain . . .

The names of boxers! *Machismo* as sheer poetry.

Though we had, in another era, "Gentleman Jim" Corbett (world heavyweight champion, 1892–97); and the first black heavyweight champion, Jack Johnson (1908–15) called himself "Li'l Arthur" as a way of commenting playfully on his powerful physique and savage ring style. (Johnson was a white man's nightmare: the black man who mocked his white opponents as he humiliated them with his fists.) In more recent times we had "Sugar Ray" Robinson and his younger namesake "Sugar Ray" Leonard. And Tyrone Crawley, a thinking man's boxer, calls himself "The Butterfly." But for the most part a boxer's ring name is chosen to suggest something more ferocious: Jack Dempsey of Manassa, Colorado, was "The Manassa Mauler"; the formidable Harry Greb was "The Human Windmill"; Joe Louis was, of course, "The Brown Bomber"; Rocky Marciano, "The Brockton Blockbuster"; Jake LaMotta, "The Bronx Bull"; Tommy Jackson, "Hurricane" Jackson; Roberto Durán, "Hands of Stone" and "The Little Killer" variously. More recent are Ray "Boom-Boom" Mancini, Thomas "Hit-Man" Hearns, James "Hard Rock" Green, Al "Earthquake" Carter, Frank "The Animal" Fletcher, Donald "The Cobra" Curry, Aaron "The Hawk" Pryor, "Terrible" Tim Witherspoon, "Bonecrusher" Smith, Johnny "Bump City" Bumphus, Lonnie "Lightning" Smith, Barry "The Clones Cyclone" McGuigan, Gene "Mad Dog" Hatcher, Livingstone "Pit Bull" Bramble, Hector "Macho Man" Camacho. "Marvelous" Marvin Hagler changed his name legally to Marvelous Marvin Hagler before his fight with Thomas Hearns brought him to national prominence.

It was once said by José Torres that the *machismo* of boxing is a condition of poverty. But it is not, surely, a condition uniquely of poverty? Or even of adolescence? I think of it as the obverse of the feminine, the denial of the feminine-in-man that has its ambiguous attractions for all men, however "civilized." It is a remnant of another, earlier era when the physical being was primary and the warrior's masculinity its highest expression.

We fighters understand lies. What's a feint?
What's a left hook off the jab?
What's an opening? What's thinking one thing
and doing another . . . ?
—José Torres,
former light-heavyweight champion of the world

One of the primary things boxing is about is lying. It's about systematically cultivating a double personality: the self in society, the self in the ring. As the chess grandmaster channels his powerful aggressive impulses onto the game board, which is the world writ small, so the "born" boxer channels his strength into the ring, against the Opponent. And in the ring, if he is a good boxer and not a mere journeyman, he will cultivate yet another split personality, to thwart the Opponent's game plan vis-à-vis *him*. Boxers, like chess players, must think on their feet—must be able to improvise in mid-fight, so to speak.

(And surely it is championship chess, and not boxing, that is our most dangerous game—at least so far as psychological risk is concerned. Megalomania and psychosis frequently await the grand master when his extraordinary mental powers can no longer be discharged onto the chessboard.)

After his upset victory against WBC junior welterweight Billy Costello in August 1985 the virtually unknown "Lightning" Lonnie Smith told an interviewer for *The Ring* that his model for boxing was that of a chess game: boxing is a "game of control, and, as in chess, this control can radiate in circles *from* the center, or in circles *toward* the center . . . The entire action of a fight goes in a circle; it can be little circles in the middle of the ring or big circles along the ropes, but always a circle. The man who wins is the man who controls the action of the circle." Smith's ring style against Costello was so brazenly idiosyncratic—reminiscent at moments of both Muhammad Ali and Jersey Joe Walcott—that the hitherto undefeated Costello, known as a hard puncher, was totally demoralized, outclassed, outboxed. (As he was outfought some months later by a furious Alexis Arguello, who "retired" Costello from the ring.)

Cassius Clay / Muhammad Ali, that most controversial of champions, was primarily a brilliant ring strategist, a prodigy in his youth whose fast hands and feet made him virtually impossible for opponents to hit. What joy in the young Ali: in the inimitable arrogance of a heavyweight who danced about his puzzled opponents with his gloves at waist level, inviting them to hit him—to try it. (What joy, at any rate, in the Ali of films and tapes, even if in somber juxtaposition to the Ali of the present time, overweight, even puffy, his speech and reactions slowed by Parkinson's disease.) It was the young boxer's style when confronted with a "deadly" puncher like Sonny Liston to simply out-think and -maneuver him: never before, and never since, has a heavyweight performed in the ring with such style—an inimitable combination of intelligence, wit, grace, irreverence, cunning. So dazzlingly talented was Ali in his youth that it wasn't clear whether in fact he had what boxers call "heart"—the ability to keep fighting when one has been hurt. In later years, when Ali's speed was diminished, a new and more complex, one might say a greater, boxer emerged, as in the trilogy of fights with Joe Frazier, the first of which Ali lost.

Sugar Ray Leonard, the most charismatic of post-Ali boxers, cultivated a ring style that was a quicksilver balance of opposites, with an overlay of street-wise, playful arrogance (reminiscent, indeed, of Ali), and, for all Leonard's talent, it was only in his most arduous matches (with Hearns and Durán) that it became clear how intelligently ferocious a boxer he really was. Losing once to Durán, he could not lose a second time: his pride would not allow it. Just as pride would not allow Leonard to continue boxing when he suspected he had passed his peak. (Though at the time of this writing Leonard has publicly declared that he wants to return for one major match: *he* is the only man who knows how to beat Marvin Hagler. A matter of ego, Leonard says, as if we needed to be told.)

The self in society, the self in the ring. But there are many selves and there are of course many boxers—ranging from the shy, introverted, painfully inarticulate Johnny Owen (the Welsh bantamweight who died after a bout with Lupe Pintor in 1979) to the frequently manic Muhammad Ali in his prime (Ali whom Norman Mailer compared to a six-foot parrot who keeps screaming at you that he is the center of the stage: "Come here and get me, fool. You can't, 'cause you don't know who I am"); from the legendary bluster of John L. Sullivan to the relative modesty of Rocky Marciano and Floyd Patterson. (Patterson, the youngest man to win the heavyweight title, is said to have been a non-violent person who once helped an opponent pick up his mouthpiece from the canvas. "I don't like to see blood," Patterson explained. "It's different when I bleed, that doesn't bother me because I can't see it." He was no match physically or otherwise for the next heavyweight champion, Sonny Liston.) For every boxer with the reputation of a Roberto Durán there are surely a dozen who are simply "nice guys"—Ray Mancini, Milton McCory, Mark Breland, Gene Hatcher, among many others. Before he lost decisive matches and began the downward trajectory of his career the young Chicago middleweight John Collins was frequently promoted as a veritable split personality, a "Dr. Jekyll / Mr. Hyde" of the ring: the essential (and surely disingenuous) question being, How can a nice courteous young man like you turn so vicious in the ring? Collins's answer was straightforward enough: "When I'm in the ring I'm fighting for my life."

It might be theorized that fighting activates in certain people not only an adrenaline rush of exquisite pleasure but an atavistic self that, coupled with an instinctive sort of tissue-intelligence, a neurological swiftness unknown to "average" men and women, makes for the born fighter, the potentially great champion, the *unmistakably* gifted boxer. An outlaw or non-law self, given the showy accolade "killer instinct." (Though to speak of instinct is always to speak vaguely: for how can "instinct" be isolated from the confluence of factors—health, economic class, familial relations, sheer good or bad luck—that determine a life?) You know the boxer with the killer instinct when the crowd jumps to its feet in a ground swell of delirium in response to his assault against his opponent, no matter if the opponent is the favorite, a "nice guy" no one really wants to see seriously injured.

There is an instinct in our species to fight but is there an instinct to *kill*? And would a "born" killer have the discipline, let alone the moral integrity, to subordinate himself to boxing's rigors in order to exercise it? Surely there are easier ways: we read about them in the daily newspaper. That the fighter, like the crowd he embodies, responds excitedly to the sight of blood—"first blood" being a term from the days of the English Prize Ring— goes without saying; but there are often fight fans shouting for a match to be stopped at the very zenith of the action. My sense of the boxing crowd in a large arena like Madison Square Garden is that it resembles a massive wave containing counter-waves, counter-currents, isolated but bold voices that resist the greater motion toward ecstatic violence. These dissenters are severely critical of referees who allow fights to go on too long.

(I seem to recall my father urging a fight to be stopped: "It's over! It's over! What's the point!" Was it Marciano battering an opponent into submission, or Carmen Basilio? Kid Gavilan? A long time ago, and in our home, the bloody match broadcast over television, hence sanitized. One cannot really imagine the impact of blows on another man's head and body by way of the television screen in its eerily flattened dimensions . . . .)

Granted these points, it is nonetheless true that the boxer who functions as a conduit through which the inchoate aggressions of the crowd are consummated will be a very popular boxer indeed. Not the conscientious "boxing" matches but the cheek-by-jowl brawls are likely to be warmly recalled in boxing legend: Dempsey-Firpo, Louis-Schmeling II, Zale-Graziano, Robinson-LaMotta, Pep-Saddler, Marciano-Charles, Ali-Frazier, most recently Hagler-Hearns. Sonny Liston occupies a position *sui generis* for the very truculence of his boxing persona——the air of unsmiling menace he presented to the Negro no less than the white world. (Liston was arrested nineteen times and served two prison terms, the second term for armed robbery.) It may be that former champion Larry Holmes saw himself in this role, the black man's black man empowered by sheer bitterness to give hurt where hurt is due. And, for a while, the Rastafarian Livingstone Bramble, whose vendetta with Ray Mancini seems to have sprung from an unmotivated ill will.

The only self-confessed murderer of boxing distinction seems to have been the welterweight champion Don Jordan (1958–60) who claimed to have been a hired assassin as a boy in his native Dominican Republic. "What's wrong with killing a human?" Jordan asked rhetorically in an interview. "The first time you kill someone, you throw up, you get sick as a dog . . . The second time, no feeling." According to his testimony Jordan killed or helped to kill more than thirty men in the Dominican Republic, without being caught. (He seems in fact to have been in the hire of the government.) After Jordan and his family moved to California he killed a man for "personal" reasons, for which crime he was sent to reform school, aged fourteen: "I burned a man like an animal . . . I staked him to the ground. I wired his hands and his arms, and I put paper around him and I burnt him like an animal. They said, 'You are mentally sick.' " In reform school Jordan was taught how to box: entered the Golden Gloves tournament and won all his matches, and eventually competed in the Olympics, where he did less well. Under the aegis of the Cosa Nostra he turned professional and his career, though meteoric, was short-lived.

In Jake LaMotta's autobiography *Raging Bull* LaMotta attributes his success as a boxer—he was middle-

weight champion briefly, 1949–51, but a popular fighter for many years—to the fact that he didn't care whether he was killed in the ring. For eleven years he mistakenly believed he had murdered a man in a robbery, and, un-confessed, yet guilty, wanting to be punished, LaMotta threw himself into boxing as much to be hurt as to hurt. His background parallels Rocky Graziano's—they were friends, as boys, in reform school—but his desperation was rather more intense than Graziano's (whose autobiography is entitled *Somebody Up There Likes Me:* a most optimistic assumption). LaMotta said in an interview: "I would fight anybody. I didn't care who they were. I even wanted to fight Joe Louis. I just didn't care . . . But that made me win. It gave me an aggression my opponents never saw before. They would hit me. I didn't care if I got hit." When LaMotta eventually learned that his victim had not died, however, his zest for boxing waned, and his career began its abrupt decline. By way of LaMotta's con-fession and the film based fragmentarily on it, *Raging Bull*, LaMotta has entered boxing folklore: he is the flashy gutter fighter whose integrity will allow him to throw only one fight (in an era in which fights were routinely thrown), done with such ironic disdain that the boxing commission suspends his license.

Traditionally, boxing is credited with changing the lives of ghetto-born or otherwise impoverished youths. It is impossible to gauge how many boxers have in fact risen from such beginnings but one might guess it to be about 99 percent—even at the present time. (Muhammad Ali is said to have been an exception in that his background was not one of desperate poverty: which helps to account, perhaps, for Ali's early boundless confidence.) Where tennis lessons were offered in some youth centers in the Detroit area, many years ago, boxing lessons were offered in Joe Louis's and Ray Robinson's neighborhood—of course. To what purpose would poor black boys learn tennis? La-Motta, Graziano, Patterson, Liston, Hector Camacho, Mike Tyson—all learned to box in captivity, so to speak. (Liston, a more advanced criminal than the others, began taking boxing lessons while serving his second term for armed robbery in the Missouri State Penitentiary.) Boxing is the moral equivalent of war of which, in a radically different context, William James spoke, and it has the virtue—how American, this virtue!—of making a good deal of money for its practitioners and promoters, not all of whom are white.

Indeed, one of the standard arguments for *not* abolishing boxing is in fact that it provides an outlet for the rage of disenfranchised youths, mainly black or Hispanic, who can make lives for themselves by way of fighting one another instead of fighting society.

The disputable term "killer instinct" was coined in reference to Jack Dempsey in his prime: in his famous early matches with Jess Willard, Georges Carpentier, Luis Firpo ("The Wild Bull of the Pampas"), and other lesser known boxers whom he savagely and conclusively beat. Has there ever been a fighter quite like the young Dempsey?—the very embodiment, it seems, of hunger, rage, the will to do hurt; the spirit of the Western frontier come East to win his fortune. The crudest of nightmare figures, Dempsey is gradually refined into an American myth of comforting dimensions. The killer in the ring becomes the New York *restaurateur*, a business success, "the gentlest of men."

Dempsey was the ninth of eleven children born to an impoverished Mormon sharecropper and itinerant railroad worker in Colorado who soon left home, bummed his way around the mining camps and small towns of the West, began fighting for money when he was hardly more than a boy. It was said in awe of Dempsey that his very sparring partners were in danger of being seriously injured— Dempsey didn't like to share the ring with anyone. If he remains the most spectacular (and most loved) champion in history it is partly because he fought when boxing rules were rather casual by our standards; when, for instance, a boxer was allowed to strike an opponent as he struggled to his feet—as in the bizarre Willard bout, and the yet more bizarre bout with Luis Firpo, set beside which present-day heavyweight matches like those of Holmes and Spinks are minuets. Where aggression has to be cultivated in some champion boxers (Tunney, for example) Dempsey's aggression was direct and natural: in the ring, he seems to have wanted to kill his opponent. The swiftness of his attack, his disdain for strategies of defense, endeared him to greatly aroused crowds who had never seen anything quite like him before.

(Dempsey's first title fight, in 1919, against the aging champion Jess Willard, was called at the time "pugilistic murder" and would certainly be stopped in the first round —in the first thirty seconds of the first round—today. Badly out of condition, heavier than the twenty-four-year-old Dempsey by seventy pounds, the thirty-seven-year-old Willard put up virtually no defense against the challenger. Though films of the match show an astonishing resilient, if not foolhardy, Willard picking himself up off the canvas repeatedly as Dempsey knocks him down, by the end of the fight Willard's jaw was broken, his cheekbone split, nose smashed, six teeth broken off at the gum, an eye was battered shut, much damage done to his lower body. Both boxers were covered in Willard's blood. Years later Dempsey's estranged manager Kearns confessed, perhaps fraudulently, that he had "loaded" Dempsey's gloves—treated his hand tape with a talcum substance that turned hard as concrete when wet.)

It was Dempsey's ring style—swift, pitiless, always direct and percussive—that changed American boxing forever. Even Jack Johnson appears stately by contrast.

So far as "killer instinct" is concerned Joe Louis was an anomaly, which no biography of his life—even the most recent, the meticulously researched *Champion—Joe Louis, Black Hero in White America* by Chris Mead—has ever quite explained. If, indeed, one can explain any of our motives, except in the most sweeping psychological and sociological terms. Louis was a modest and self-effacing man outside the ring, but, in the ring, a machine of sorts for hitting—so (apparently) emotionless that even sparring partners were spooked by him. "It's the eyes," one said. "They're blank and staring, always watching you. That blank look—that's what gets you down." Unlike his notorious predecessor Jack Johnson and his yet more notorious successor Muhammad Ali, Joe Louis was forced to live his "blackness" in secret, if at all; to be a *black* hero in *white* America at the time of Louis's coming-of-age cannot have been an easy task. Louis's deadpan expression and his killer's eyes were very likely aspects of the man's strategy rather than reliable gauges of his psyche. And his descent into mental imbalance—paranoia, in particular—in his later years was surely a consequence of the pressures he endured, if not an outsized, but poetically valid, response to the very real scrutiny of others focused upon him for decades.

One of the most controversial of boxing legends has to do with the death of Benny "Kid" Paret at the hands of Emile Griffith in a welterweight match in Madison Square Garden in 1962. According to the story Paret provoked Griffith at their weigh-in by calling him *maricón* (faggot), and was in effect killed by Griffith in the ring that night. Recalling the event years later Griffith said he was only following his trainer's instructions—to hit Paret, to hurt Paret, to keep punching Paret until the referee made him stop. By which time, as it turned out, Paret was virtually dead. (He died about ten days later.)

Though there are other boxing experts, present at the

match, who insist that Paret's death was accidental: it "just happened."

At the present time boxing matches are usually monitored by referees and ringside physicians with extreme caution: a recent match between welterweights Don Curry and James Green was stopped by the referee because Green, temporarily disabled, had lowered his gloves and *might have been hit;* a match between heavyweights Mike Weaver and Michael Dokes was stopped within two minutes of the first round, before the luckless Weaver had time to begin. With some exceptions—the Sandoval-Canizales and the Bramble-Crawley title fights come most immediately to mind—referees have been assuming ever greater authority in the ring so that it sometimes seems that the drama of boxing has begun to shift: not will X knock out his opponent, but will the referee stop the fight before he can do so. In the most violent fights the predominant image is that of the referee hovering at the periphery of the action, stepping in to embrace a weakened or defenseless man in a gesture of paternal solicitude. This image carries much emotional power—not so sensational as the killing blow but suggestive, perhaps, that the ethics of the ring have evolved to approximate the ethics of everyday life. It is as if, in mythical terms, brothers whose mysterious animosity has brought them to battle are saved—absolved of their warriors' enmity—by the wisdom of their father and protector. One came away from the eight-minute Hagler-Hearns fight with the vision of the dazed Hearns, on his feet but not fully conscious, saved by referee Richard Steele from what would have been serious injury, if not death—considering the extraordinary ferocity of Hagler's fighting that night, and the personal rage he seems to have brought to it. ("This was war," Hagler said.) The fight ends with Hearns in Steele's embrace: tragedy narrowly averted.

Of course there are many who disdain such developments. It's the *feminization* of the sport, they say.

I was never knocked out. I've been unconscious,
but it's always been on my feet.
—FLOYD PATTERSON,
former heavyweight champion of the world

No American sport or activity has been so consistently and so passionately under attack as boxing, for "moral" as well as other reasons. And no American sport evokes so ambivalent a response in its defenders: when asked the familiar question "How can you watch . . . ?" the boxing *aficionado* really has no answer. He can talk about boxing only with others like himself.

In December 1984 the American Medical Association passed a resolution calling for the abolition of boxing

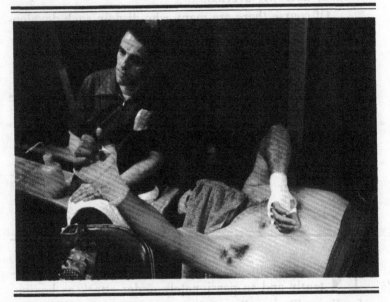

for "moral" as well as other reasons. And no American sport evokes so ambivalent a response in its defenders: when asked the familiar question "How can you watch ...?", the boxing aficionado really has no answer. He can talk about boxing only with others like himself.

In December 1984 the American Medical Association passed a resolution calling for the abolition of boxing

on the principle that while other sports involve as much,
or even more, risk to life and health—the most dangerous
sports being football, auto racing, hang gliding, mountain
climbing, and ice hockey, with boxing in about seventh
place—boxing is the only sport in which the objective is
to cause injury: the brain is the target, the knockout the
goal. In one study it was estimated that 87 percent of
boxers suffer some degree of brain damage in their life-
times, no matter the relative success of their careers. And
there is the risk of serious eye injury as well. Equally
disturbing, though less plausible, is sociological evidence
that media attention focused on boxing has an immediate
effect upon the homicide rate of the country. (According to
sociologists David P. Phillips and John E. Hensley, the
rate rises by an average of 12 percent in the days following a highly publicized fight, for the hypothetical reason
that the fight "heavily rewards one person for inflicting
violence on another and is at the opposite end of a contin-
uum from a successfully prosecuted murder trial, which
heavily punishes one person for inflicting physical violence on another.") Doubtful as these findings are in a
culture in which television and movie violence has become
routine fare, even for young children, it does seem likely
that boxing as a phenomenon *sui generis* stimulates rather
than resolves certain emotions. If boxing is akin to classic
tragedy in its imitation of action and of life it cannot
provide the *katharsis* of pity and terror of which Aristotle
spoke.

The variegated history of boxing reform is very

likely as old as boxing itself. As I mentioned earlier, in the days of Pierce Egan's *Boxiana* the Prize Ring was in fact outlawed in England—though the aristocracy, including the Prince Regent, regularly attended matches. Boxing has been intermittently illegal in various parts of the United States and campaigns are frequently launched to ban it altogether. Like abortion it seems to arouse deep and divisive emotions. (Though activists who would outlaw abortion are not necessarily those who would outlaw boxing: puritanical instincts take unpredictable forms.) The relationship between boxing and poverty is acknowledged, but no one suggests that poverty be abolished as the most practical means of abolishing boxing. So frequently do young boxers claim they are in greater danger on the street than in the ring that one has to assume they are not exaggerating for the sake of credulous white reporters.

It is objected too that boxing as a sport is closely bound up with organized crime. Investigations on the federal and state level, over the decades, but most prominently in the fifties, have made the connection unmistakable, though the situation at any time is problematic. One wonders about "suspicious" decisions—are they fixed, or simply the consequence of judges' prejudices? As in Michael Spinks's second, highly controversial win over Larry Holmes, for instance; and the Wilfredo Gomez–Rocky Lockridge match of May 1985 (when judges gave a world junior-lightweight title to a Puerto Rican hometown favorite). And recent televised performances by former

Olympic Gold Medalists and their handpicked opponents have struck the eye of more than one observer as not entirely convincing . . .

Not long ago I saw a film of a long-forgotten fixed fight of Willie Pep's in which Pep allowed himself to be overcome by an underdog opponent: the great featherweight performed as a boxer-turned-actor might be expected to perform, with no excess of zeal or talent. It occurred to me that boxing is so refined, yet so raw a sport that no match can be successfully thrown; the senses simply pick up on what is not happening, what is being held back, as a sort of ironic subtext to what is actually taking place. You can run but you can't hide.

Not boxing in itself but the money surrounding it, the gambling in Las Vegas, Atlantic City, and elsewhere, is the problem, and a problem not likely to be solved. I have made an attempt to read the 135-page single-spaced document "Organized Crime in Boxing: Final Boxing Report of the State of New Jersey Commission of Investigation" of December 1985 and have come to the conclusion that the Commission, which has moved to abolish boxing in New Jersey, was wrongheaded in its initial approach: it should have been investigating organized crime in New Jersey, in which Atlantic City boxing/gambling figures. That the Commission would vote to abolish boxing altogether because of criminal connections suggests a naïveté shading into sheer vindictiveness: one would then be required to abolish funeral parlors, pizzerias, trucking firms, some labor unions. And if gamblers can't gamble on boxing they will simply gamble on football, basketball, baseball—as they already do.

Since boxing has become a multimillion-dollar business under the aegis of a few canny promoters—the most visible being Don King—it is not likely that it will be abolished, in any case. It would simply be driven underground, like abortion; or exiled to Mexico, Cuba, Canada, England, Ireland, Zaire . . . Boxing's history is one of such exigencies, fascinating for what they suggest of the compulsion of some men to fight and of others to be witnesses.

The 1896 heavyweight title match between Ruby Robert Fitzsimmons and Peter Maher, for instance, was outlawed everywhere in the States, so promoters staged it on an isolated sandbar in the Rio Grande River, four hundred miles from El Paso. (Can one imagine?—three hundred men made the arduous journey to witness what was surely one of the most disappointing title bouts in boxing history when Fitzsimmons knocked out Maher in ninety-five seconds.) During Jack Dempsey's prime in the 1920s boxing was outlawed in a number of states, like alcohol, and, like alcohol, seems to have aroused a hysterical public enthusiasm. Dempsey's notorious five minutes with the giant Argentinian Firpo was attended by eighty-five thousand people—most of whom could barely have seen the ring, let alone the boxers; both Dempsey's fights with Gene Tunney were attended by over a hundred thousand people—the first fought in a downpour during which rain fell in "blinding sheets" for forty minutes on both boxers and onlookers alike. Photographs of these events show jammed arenas with boxing rings like postage-sized altars at their centers, the boxers themselves no more than tiny, heraldic figures. To attend a Dempsey match was not to have seen a Dempsey match, but perhaps that was not the issue.

When Jack Johnson won the heavyweight title in 1908 he had to pursue the white champion Tommy Burns all the way to Australia to confront him. The "danger" of boxing at that time—and one of the reasons worried citizens wanted to abolish it—was that it might expose and humiliate white men in the ring. After Johnson's decisive victory over the White Hope contender Jim Jeffries there were in fact race riots and lynchings throughout the United States; even films of some of Johnson's fights were outlawed in many states. And because in recent decades boxing has become a sport in which black and Hispanic men have excelled it is particularly vulnerable to attack by white middle-class reformers (the AMA in particular) who show very little interest in lobbying against equally dangerous Establishment sports like football, auto racing, thoroughbred horse racing.

The late Nat Fleischer, boxing expert and founder of *The Ring* magazine, once estimated that tens of thousands of injuries have occurred in the ring since the start of modern boxing in the 1890s—by "modern" meaning the introduction of the rules of the Marquis of Queensberry requiring padded gloves, three-minute rounds, one min-

ute's rest between rounds, continuous fighting during
rounds. (The bare-knuckle era, despite its popular reputation for brutality, was far less dangerous for fighters—fists
break more readily than heads.) Between 1945 and 1985
at least three hundred seventy boxers have died in the
United States of injuries directly attributed to boxing. In
addition to the infamous Griffith-Paret fight there have
been a number of others given wide publicity: Sugar Ray
Robinson killed a young boxer named Jimmy Doyle in
1947, for instance, while defending his welterweight title;
Sugar Ramos won the featherweight title in 1963 by
knocking out the champion Davey Moore, who never
regained consciousness; Ray Mancini killed the South Korean Duk Koo-Kim in 1982; former featherweight champion Barry McGuigan killed the Nigerian "Young Ali" in
1983. After the death of Duk Koo-Kim the World Boxing
Council shortened title bouts to twelve rounds. (The World
Boxing Association retains fifteen. In the era of marathon
fights, however—1892 to 1915—men often fought as
many as one hundred rounds; the record is one hundred
ten, in 1893, over a stupefying seven-hour period. The
last scheduled forty-five-round championship fight was between the black title-holder Jack Johnson and his White
Hope successor Willard in 1915: the match went twenty-
six rounds beneath a blazing sun in Havana, Cuba, before
Johnson collapsed.)

To say that the rate of death and injury in the ring is
not extraordinary set beside the rates of other sports is to
misread the nature of the criticism brought to bear against

boxing (and not against other sports). Clearly, boxing's very image is repulsive to many people because it cannot be assimilated into what we wish to know about civilized man. In a technological society possessed of incalculably refined methods of mass destruction (consider how many times over both the United States and the Soviet Union have vaporized each other in fantasy) boxing's display of direct and unmitigated and seemingly natural aggression is too explicit to be tolerated.

Which returns us to the paradox of boxing: its obsessive appeal for many who find in it not only a spectacle involving sensational feats of physical skill but an emotional experience impossible to convey in words; an art form, as I've suggested, with no natural analogue in the arts. Of course it is primitive, too, as birth, death, and erotic love might be said to be primitive, and forces our reluctant acknowledgment that the most profound experiences of our lives are physical events—though we believe ourselves to be, and surely are, essentially spiritual beings.

I ain't never liked violence.
—*SUGAR RAY ROBINSON,*
**former welterweight and
middleweight champion of the world**

To the untrained eye most boxing matches appear not merely savage but mad. As the eye becomes trained, however, the spectator begins to see the complex patterns that underlie the "madness"; what seems to be merely confusing action is understood to be coherent and intelligent, frequently inspired. Even the spectator who dislikes violence in principle can come to admire highly skillful boxing—to admire it beyond all "sane" proportions. A brilliant boxing match, quicksilver in its motions, transpiring far more rapidly than the mind can absorb, can have the power that Emily Dickinson attributed to great poetry: you know it's great when it takes the top of your head off. (The physical imagery Dickinson employs is peculiarly apt in this context.)

This early impression—that boxing is "mad," or mimics the actions of madness—seems to me no less valid, however, for being, by degrees, substantially modi-

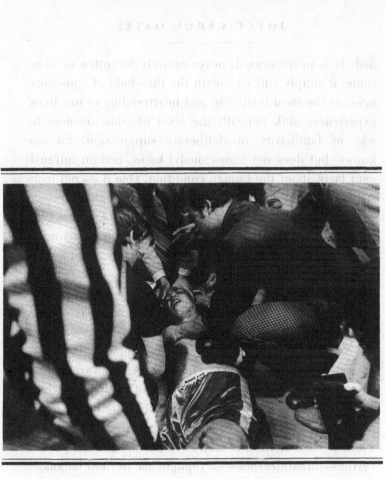

fied. It is never erased, never entirely forgotten or overcome; it simply sinks beneath the threshold of consciousness, as the most terrifying and heartrending of our lives'
experiences sink beneath the level of consciousness by
way of familiarity or deliberate suppression. So one
knows, but does not (consciously) know, certain intransigent facts about the human condition. One does not (consciously) know, but one *knows*. All boxing fans, however
accustomed to the sport, however many decades have
been invested in their obsession, know that boxing is
sheerly madness, for all its occasional beauty. That knowledge is our common bond and sometimes—dare it be uttered?—our common shame.

To watch boxing closely, and seriously, is to risk
moments of what might be called animal panic—a sense
not only that something very ugly is happening but that,
by watching it, one is an accomplice. This awareness, or
revelation, or weakness, or hairline split in one's cuticle of
a self can come at any instant, unanticipated and unbid-
den; though of course it tends to sweep over the viewer
when he is watching a really violent match. I feel it as
vertigo—breathlessness—a repugnance beyond language:
a sheerly physical loathing. That it is also, or even primarily, self-loathing goes without saying.

For boxing really isn't metaphor, it is the thing in
itself. And my predilection for watching matches on tape,
when the outcomes are known, doesn't alter the fact that,
as the matches occurred, they occurred in the present

tense, and for one time only. The rest is subterfuge—the intellectual's uneasy "control" of his material.

Impossible to see the old, early fights of Dempsey's and not to feel this *frisson* of dread, despite the poor quality of the films, the somewhat antic rhythms of the human figures. Or, I would guess, the trilogy of Zale-Graziano fights about which people speak in awe forty years later. For one man of my acquaintance it was a fight of Joe Louis's, against a long-forgotten opponent. For another, one of the "great" dirty matches of Willie Pep and Sandy Saddler—"little white perfection / and death in red plaid trunks" as the poet Philip Levine has written of that infamous duo. There was Duk Koo-Kim, there was Johnny Owen, in an earlier decade luckless Benny Paret, trapped in the ropes as referee Ruby Goldstein stood frozen, unable to interfere—

And Paret? Paret died on his feet. As he took those eighteen punches something happened to everyone who was in psychic range of the event. Some part of his death reached out to us. One felt it hover in the air. He was still standing in the ropes, trapped as he had been before, he gave some little half-smile of regret, as if he were saying, "I didn't know I was going to die just yet," and then, his head leaning back but still erect, his death came to breathe about him. He began to pass away. He went down more slowly than any fighter had ever gone down, he went down like a large ship which turns on end and slides second by second into its grave.

As he went down, the sound of Griffith's punches echoed in the mind like a heavy ax in the distance chopping into a wet log.

(NORMAN MAILER, *"Ten Thousand Words a Minute"*)

For one friend of mine it was a bloody fight fought by the lightweight contender Bobby Chacon that filled him with horror—though, ironically, Chacon came back to win the match (as Chacon was once apt to do). For another friend, a fellow novelist, enamored of boxing since boyhood, it was the Hagler-Hearns fight of 1985—he was frightened by his own ecstatic participation in it.

At such times one thinks: What is happening? why are we here? what does this mean? can't this be stopped? My terror at seeing Floyd Patterson battered into insensibility by Sonny Liston was not assuaged by my rational understanding that the event had taken place long ago and that, in fact, Patterson is in fine health at the present time, training an adopted son to box. (Liston of course has been dead for years—he died of a heroin overdose, aged thirty-eight, in "suspicious" circumstances.) More justified, perhaps, was my sickened sense that boxing is, simply, wrong, a mistake, an outlaw activity for some reason under the protectorate of the law, when, a few weeks ago in March 1986, I sat in the midst of a suddenly very quiet closed-circuit television audience in a suburban Trenton hall watching bantamweight Richie Sandoval as he lay flat and unmoving on his back . . . very likely dead of a savage beating the referee had not, for some reason, stopped in time. My conviction was that anything was preferable to boxing, anything was preferable to seeing another minute of it, for instance standing outside in the parking lot for the remainder of the evening and staring at the stained asphalt . . . .

A friend who is a sportswriter was horrified by the same fight. In a letter he spoke of his intermittent disgust for the sport he has been watching most of his life, and writing about for years: "It's all a bit like bad love— putting up with the pain, waiting for the sequel to the last good moment. And like bad love, there comes the point of being worn out, when the reward of the good moment doesn't seem worth all the trouble . . . ."

Yet we don't give up on boxing, it isn't that easy. Perhaps it's like tasting blood. Or, more discreetly put, love commingled with hate is more powerful than love. Or hate.

The spectacle of human beings fighting each other for whatever reason, including, at certain well-publicized times, staggering sums of money, is enormously disturbing because it violates a taboo of our civilization. Many men and women, however they steel themselves, cannot watch a boxing match because they cannot allow themselves to see what it is they are seeing. One thinks helplessly, This can't be happening, even as, and usually quite routinely, it *is* happening. In this way boxing as a public spectacle is akin to pornography: in each case the spectator is made a voyeur, distanced, yet presumably intimately involved, in an event that is not supposed to be happening as it is happening. The pornographic "drama," though as fraudulent as professional wrestling, makes a claim for being about something absolutely serious, if not humanly profound: it is not so much about itself as about the violation of a taboo. That the taboo is spiritual rather than physical, or sexual—that our most valuable human experience, love, is being desecrated, parodied, mocked— is surely at the core of our culture's fascination with pornography. In another culture, undefined by spiritual-emotional values, pornography could not exist, for who would pay to see it?

The obvious difference between boxing and pornography is that boxing, unlike pornography, is not theatrical. It is not, except in instances so rare as to be irrelevant, rehearsed or simulated. Its violation of the taboo against violence ("Thou shalt not kill" in its primordial form) is open, explicit, ritualized, and, as I've said, *routine* —which gives boxing its uncanny air. Unlike pornography (and professional wrestling) it is altogether real: the blood shed, the damage suffered, the pain (usually suppressed or sublimated) are unfeigned. Not for hemophobics, boxing is a sport in which blood becomes quickly irrelevant. The experienced viewer understands that a boxer's bleeding face is probably the least of his worries, and may, in fact, mean nothing at all—one thinks of Rocky Marciano's garishly bloodied but always triumphant face, Marvin Hagler's forehead streaming blood even as he outfought Thomas Hearns. The severely bleeding boxer and his seconds are anxious not about his cut face but about the possibility of the fight being stopped, which means a TKO victory for the opponent. Recall Ray "Boom Boom" Mancini in his second match with Livingstone Bramble, in which he desperately tried to wipe away with his gloves blood pouring from inch-long cuts in his eyelids: twenty-seven stitches were needed to sew up the cuts afterward. (Bramble, pragmatic like all boxers, naturally worked Mancini's damaged eyes as frequently as he could. Of 674 blows struck by Bramble 255 struck him in the face.)

Just as the boxer is trained to fight until he can't go on, so he is trained, or is by nature equipped, to fight unconscious on his feet. The image is indelibly imprinted in my memory of the doomed South Korean lightweight Duk Koo-Kim struggling to rise from the canvas after a blow of Mancini's burst a blood vessel in his brain—as if his body possessed its own demonic will even at the threshold of death. It is said that Joe Louis, badly stunned by Max Schmeling in their first fight, fought unconscious for several rounds—his beautifully conditioned body performing its trained motions like clockwork. (And it was during this losing bout that Louis's prodigious talent for endurance, and therefore for great boxing, manifested itself.) So customary is this sort of "fearless" boxing that the behavior of heavyweight Jesse Ferguson in his February 1986 match with Mike Tyson—clinching, holding on to Tyson's gloves, refusing in effect to fight—struck the eye as unnatural when of course it was utterly natural, the way the average man would behave in so desperate a situation. But boxing is contrary to nature.

One of the paradoxes of boxing is that the viewer inhabits a consciousness so very different from that of the boxer as to suggest a counter-world. "Free" will, "sanity," "rationality"—our characteristic modes of consciousness —are irrelevant, if not detrimental, to boxing in its most extraordinary moments. Even as he disrobes himself ceremonially in the ring the great boxer must disrobe himself of both reason and instinct's caution as he prepares to fight.

Dustin Hoffman recalls a boxing match he had seen as a boy: as the triumphant boxer left the ring to pass up the aisle, an ecstatic fight fan, male, followed closely after him, wiping all he could of the sweat from the boxer's body onto himself.

An observer is struck by boxing's intense preoccupation with its own history; its continuous homage to a gallery of heroes—or are they saints? At Muhammad Ali's Deer Lake, Pennsylvania, training camp the names of heavyweight champions—Louis, Marciano, Liston, Patterson, et al.—were painted in white letters on massive iconographic boulders. "Jack Dempsey" named himself for the middleweight champion Jack Dempsey (1884–91 —known as Dempsey "The Nonpareil" because he outboxed every man he fought). "Sugar Ray" Leonard named himself boldly after "Sugar Ray" Robinson—an act of audacity that did not prove embarrassing. If Marvin Hagler shaves his head, the image of Rubin "Hurricane" Carter comes to mind, and, beyond him, that of Jack Johnson himself—the first and very likely the greatest of defiantly *black* boxers, whom Cassius Clay / Muhammad Ali admired as well. So frequently are a few names evoked— Dempsey, Louis, Marciano, Pep, Robinson—one might think these boxers were our contemporaries and not champions of eras long past.

If boxing exhausts most of its practitioners in a Darwinian struggle for survival like virtually no other, it so honors a very few, so enshrines them in the glamour of immortality, surely the danger is justified? As in any religion, present and past are magically one; Time, even death, are defeated. The dead immortals are always with us, not only their names and the hazy outlines of careers recalled, but individual bouts, moments when decisive punches were thrown and caught, the size of a boxer's fist, the measurement of his reach, his age when he began and when he retired, his record of wins, losses, draws. The uppercut Jack Johnson used against Stanley Ketchel in 1909—the famous Fitzsimmons "shift" of 1897 (when

Fitzsimmons defeated Gentleman Jim Corbett for the heavyweight title)—the wicked left hook with which Jack Dempsey caught a distracted Jack Sharkey in 1927—Rocky Marciano's several right-hand knockout punches—Cassius Clay's mystery punch in the first minute of the first round of his second match with Sonny Liston—the left hook of Joe Frazier that knocked Muhammad Ali on his back in the fifteenth round of their first fight: all are commemorated. The typical boxing writer's imagination is not so much stimulated by his subject as enflamed. Dream matches are routinely fantasized in which boxers of different eras meet one another—Marciano-Dempsey, Louis-Ali, Hagler-Robinson, the 1961 Sonny Liston and the 1973 George Foreman. Boxers of different weights are thrown together—how would Willie Pep or Benny Leonard or Roberto Durán have done against Joe Louis, *equipped with the necessary poundage?* Though preoccupation with past records is common to most sports there is something unusually intense about it in boxing, perhaps because, in boxing, the individual is so very alone, or seems so. Like the saint he gives the impression of having arrived at his redemption by unflagging solitary effort.

The boxing past exists in an uncannily real and vital relationship with the present. The dead are not dead, or not merely dead. When, for instance, Larry Holmes made his ill-advised attempt to equal Rocky Marciano's record (forty-nine wins, no losses) it seemed suddenly that Marciano was living again, his name and photograph in all the papers, interviews with his family published. Michael

Spinks resurrected not only Billy Conn, the light-heavy-weight champion who was defeated in a famous match by Joe Louis in 1941 (and again in 1946) but any number of other light-heavyweight champions who were defeated by heavyweight champions—Georges Carpentier, Tommy Loughran, Joey Maxim, the indefatigable Archie Moore. The spectacular first round of the Hagler-Hearns match provoked reminiscences of "the greatest first rounds of all time." (Number one remains Dempsey-Firpo, 1923.) *The Ring*'s Hall of Fame—to which controversial Jake La-Motta was only recently elected—corresponds to the pantheon of saints elected by the Vatican except it is in fact more finely calibrated, its saints arranged under various groupings and subgroupings, and its balloting highly complex. (Indeed, no intellectual journal in the States is more scrupulously attentive to its history than this famous boxing magazine, founded by Nat Fleischer in 1922, in which past, present, and a hypothesized future are tirelessly examined, and in which one finds articles on such subjects as "The Greatest Disappointments in Ring History," "The Greatest Mismatches," "The Greatest Left Hooks," "When a Good Little Man *Did* Defeat a Good Big Man.")

It is as if by way of the most strenuous exigencies of the physical self a boxer can—sometimes—transcend the merely physical; he can, if he is lucky, be absolved of his mortality. The instinct is of course closely allied with the desire for fame and riches (those legendary champions with their purple Cadillacs!) but is not finally identical with it. If the boxing ring is an altar it is not an altar of sacrifice solely but one of consecration and redemption. Sometimes.

". . . I am a sophomore at [an upstate New York SUNY campus] and when I'm at school I work out at a downtown gym 5 days a week. The gym is completely removed from the atmosphere of school in every way. Through boxing I manage to release aggression . . . I've yet to have my first amateur fight. My trainer says when I'm sparring I don't look like I want to hurt my man. 'You gotta want to hurt him, because he's sure going to hurt you.' I'm afraid my lack of bloodlust stems from a fear of going too far, physically and/or mentally. However far I push myself in the gym something in me is holding back . . .

"I have very little idea what it was that attracted me to boxing in the first place. No one in my immediate experience ever had the least interest in it. What started as a little fooling around at the Y soon turned into almost an obsession . . . Over Christmas break I had a bad experience I'd rather not repeat. The trainer gave me a break, said he'd let me train with the team for a while, and I wound up sparring the first night with a fellow who outmatched me pretty badly in experience. I took a 3-round beating, never letting him knock me down, but *taking plenty of punishment, mostly jabs that landed on or around my nose, which I was sure must be broken by the end of the second round. After practice the trainer told me I had a hell of a lot of heart. Don't blow your nose, he said, or your eyes will black, and be here tomorrow. Driving home I knew 'heart' meant crazy or stupid or both, but still the wave of elation I felt matched the fear and trepidation that came over me before I entered that ring . . . and afterwards anticipating facing my parents. I didn't leave the house for days after that, I became depressed and embarrassed, I thought that perhaps boxing wasn't worth it after all, maybe I couldn't cut it, and I was afraid I'd already lost whatever looks I had. My face swelled up to an unspeakably ugly apparition, and I carried two black eyes for months afterwards.*

"I took an introductory course to poetry last semester and through it I became convinced that the best way to convey my reasons for and feelings about boxing would be through poetry . . ."

—excerpts of letters to
the author from a young boxer

*If they cut my bald head open,
they will find one big boxing glove.
That's all I am. I live it.*
—MARVIN HAGLER

T hough boxing has long been popular in many coun-
tries and under many forms of government, dicta-
torships no less than democracies, surely its popularity in
the States since the days of John L. Sullivan has a good
deal to do with what Americans honor as the spirit of the
individual—his "physical" spirit—in defiance of the
State. The remarkable rise of boxing in the 1920s in particular can be seen as a consequence of the diminution of
the individual vis-à-vis society; the gradual attrition of
personal freedom, will, and strength—"masculine," to be
sure, but not solely masculine. What more appropriate
hero for the times than the pitiless ex-barroom brawler
Jack Dempsey of Manassa, Colorado? Today, the "totali-
tarian" consciousness in the Eastern bloc of nations is
clearly a function of the state while in the Western bloc it
has come to seem a function of technology, if not history
—inexorable fate. How to master these ever more difficult
machines, how even to learn their language, when so
many of us are illiterate . . . The individual exists in his
physical supremacy, but does the individual matter?

In the magical space of the boxing ring so disturbing
a question has no claim. There as in no other public arena
does the individual as a unique physical being assert himself; there, for a dramatic if fleeting period of time, the
great world with its moral and political complexities, its
terrifying impersonality, ceases to exist. Men fighting one
another with only their fists and their cunning are all
contemporaries, all brothers, belonging to no historical

time. The crowd, borne along with them, belongs to no historical time. "He can run but he can't hide"—so said Joe Louis before his great fight with Conn in 1941. In the brightly lit ring, man is *in extremis*, performing an atavistic rite or *agon* for the mysterious solace of those who can participate only vicariously in such drama: the drama of life in the flesh. Boxing has become America's tragic theater.

ON MIKE TYSON

ON MIKE TYSON

November 22, 1986. When twenty-year-old Mike Tyson enters the packed arena of the Las Vegas Hilton Convention Center, it is through a deafening wall of noise. A neutral observer would wonder: Is this young man already a champion?—a *great* champion? Of the nearly nine thousand people jammed into the arena—in seats as costly as $1,000 at ringside—virtually everyone has come in expectation of seeing not merely a heavyweight title fight that promises to be unusually dramatic but boxing history itself. If Tyson takes away the World Boxing Council heavyweight title held by thirty-three-year-old Trevor Berbick, as he has promised to do, he will become the youngest heavyweight champion in the sport's recorded history. He will fulfill the prophecy made by the late Cus D'Amato, his boxing trainer, mentor, and guardian, that he would one day break the record of another of D'Amato's heavyweight prodigies, Floyd Patterson, who won the title shortly before his twenty-second birthday in 1956.

Mike Tyson, a boy warrior, has become legendary, in a sense, before there is a legend to define him. And never has the collective will of a crowd—the very nearly palpable *wish* of a crowd—been more powerfully expressed than it is tonight in Las Vegas. With his much-publicized 27–0 record as a professional boxer, of which twenty-five victories are knockouts (fifteen in the first round, several within sixty seconds), with so much expectation centered upon him as the "new hope" of heavyweight boxing, Tyson recalls the young Jack Dempsey, who fought his most spectacular fights before wining the heavyweight title. Like Dempsey in the upward trajectory of his career, Tyson suggests a savagery only symbolically contained within the brightly illuminated elevated ring, with its referee, its resident physician, its scrupulously observed rules, regulations, customs, and rituals. Like Dempsey he has the power to galvanize crowds as if awakening in them the instinct not merely for raw aggression and the mysterious will to do hurt that resides, for better or worse, in the human soul, but for suggesting the incontestable *justice* of such an instinct: his is not the image of the Establishment-approved Olympic Gold Medalist, like Muhammad Ali or Sugar Ray Leonard (indeed, it is said in boxing circles that Tyson was cheated of a gold medal at the 1984 Summer Olympic Games by way of the politics of amateur boxing), but the image of the outsider, the psychic outlaw, the hungry young black contender for all that white America can give. In a weight division in which hard punching is the point, Tyson has acquired a reputation for being an awesome fighter, as much admired and feared among his coevals as Sonny Liston, George

Foreman, and Rocky Marciano were in their times: he has been called a "tank," a "young bull," a "killer," a "block of granite"; a force primitive and irresistible as nature. As one observer noted, there is something of a comic-book quality about Tyson's fights—the violence is so exaggerated it has a surrealist air. Opponents are propelled across the ring, fall insensible into the ropes, or, fully conscious, lose muscular control in their legs; they lie without moving for what seems a very long time. The violence may appear primitive and surrealist but it is thoughtfully administered: the result, as Tyson explains carefully in his soft, earnest, boyish voice, of punches thrown with a "bad intention in a vital area." Cus D'Amato was, among other things, a "master of anatomy."

Tyson himself has spoken of the phenomenon of Mike Tyson in gladiatorial terms: the warrior's vow to fight to the death if necessary precludes and makes irrelevant all merely personal motives, all conventional rationalizations for what he does. Boxing is his life, his vocation; his calling. The Roman boast of *munera sine missione* in the gladiatorial games—no mercy shown—would be perfectly logical to him. And so mesmerizing has the young boxer become in his scant eighteen months as a professional, his appearance in the ring tonight in Las Vegas, his mere physical *presence*, captivates the crowd's attention to the degree that the entrance of reigning WBC champion Trevor Berbick goes virtually unnoticed. Even the blazoning recorded music is abruptly and mysteriously silenced.

Mike Tyson—"Kid Dynamite" as he has lately been billed—exudes an air of tension, control, fierce concentration. At five feet eleven inches, he is short for a heavyweight and strikes the eye as shorter still; his 222¼-pound body is so sculpted in muscle it looks foreshortened, brutally compact. (Berbick, at 218½ pounds, stands six feet two inches—not a large man by today's heavyweight standards—and will have a daunting seven-inch reach advantage.) Indeed, Tyson is so muscular as to resemble a bodybuilder rather than a boxer, for whom upper-body flexibility is crucial; his neck measures an extraordinary nineteen inches—larger than any heavyweight champion's since the circus strongman Primo Carnera. His hair is trimmed savagely short, Dempsey-style, along the back and sides, as if it were done with a razor; he wears not a robe but a crude white terry-cloth pullover that looks as if he might have made it himself and, as usual, no socks—"I feel more like a warrior this way"; and though his managers Jim Jacobs and Bill Cayton will be fined $5,000 by the Nevada State Athletic Commission for the privilege, Tyson is wearing the black trunks that have become his trademark. (Trevor Berbick, who usually wears white, preempted black for *his* trunks —very likely because he resents the extraordinary pre-fight publicity Tyson has engendered and the humiliating fact that, though the young challenger has never met an opponent of Berbick's stature, he is a 3-to-1 favorite to win tonight.) Tyson remains the object of the crowd's rapt attention. He is pumped up, covered in sweat, ready to fight. Though this is the hour—the very moment—to which the past six years of his life have been subordinated, he gives no sign of nerves and will say, afterward, that he was "calm" and "relaxed" in the knowledge that he could not fail.

As he gives Tyson final instructions, his trainer, Kevin Rooney—himself a D'Amato protégé—touches foreheads with him and kisses him lightly on the cheek. (Strangers to boxing's eerie combination of violence and childlike affection are invariably startled by such gestures, as by the abruptness with which, after the final bell, boxers often embrace each other in mutual gratitude for the fight. But such behavior, as spontaneous as it is traditional, and as natural as it is apparently contradictory, lies at the very heart of boxing.) As soon as the bell sounds, opening round one, Tyson rushes out of his corner to bring the fight to Berbick. In these quicksilver seconds, when far more happens than the eye, let alone the verbalizing consciousness, can absorb, it is clear that Tyson is the stronger of the two, the more dominant; willful. He pushes forward unmindful of Berbick's greater age and experience; the fight is to be *his* fight. If boxing is as much a contest of psyches as of physical prowess, it is soon clear that Tyson, on the attack, throwing beautifully controlled punches, is the superior boxer; and he is fast —unexpectedly fast. "This kid don't let you do what you want to do," Berbick's trainer Angelo Dundee will say after the fight. "He created the pressure and my guy didn't react to the pressure. . . . He throws combinations I never saw before. When have you seen a guy throw a right hand to the kidney, come up the middle with an uppercut, then throw a left hook. He throws punches...like a trigger." (This in significant contrast to Tyson's less effective performances against José Ribalta in August 1986 and James "Quick" Tillis in May: the improvement, in so brief a period of time, is remarkable.) For those of us who have been watching preliminary bouts for the past two and a half hours, including a perfectly controlled but lackluster if not contemptuous performance by former WBC champion Pinklon Thomas, the quality of Tyson's fighting—one might say Tyson's *being*—is profound. The impact of certain of his body blows is felt in the farthest corners of the arena; the intensity of his fighting is without parallel. As an observer notes, Tyson's punches even sound different from other boxers' punches. In the ring, in the terrible intensity of action, Tyson is both sui generis and as stylized as the heraldic, struggling figures painted by George Bellows in such famous oils as "Stag at Sharkey's" and "Dempsey and Firpo." It seems suddenly possible that, as Cus D'Amato predicted, Tyson differs not merely in degree but in kind from his fellow boxers.

Early in the second round, Tyson knocks Berbick to the canvas with a powerful combination of blows, including a left hook; when Berbick manages to get gamely to his feet he is knocked down a second time with a left hook to the head—to be precise, to the right temple, a "vital area." (As Tyson will say afterward, he had come to "destroy" the champion: "Every punch had a murderous intention.") Accompanied by the wild clamor of the crowd as by an exotic sort of music, Berbick struggles to his feet, his expression glazed like that of a man trapped in a dream; he lurches across the ring on wobbly legs, falls another time, onto the ropes, as if by a sheer effort of will gets up, staggers across the ring in the opposite direction, is precariously on his feet when the referee, Mills Lane, stops the fight. No more than nine seconds have passed since Tyson's blow but the sequence, in slow motion, has seemed much longer. . . . The nightmare image of a man struggling to retain consciousness and physical control before nine thousand witnesses is likely to linger in the memory: it is an image as inevitable in boxing as that of the ecstatic boxer with his gloved hands raised in triumph.

At two minutes thirty-five seconds of the second round, the fight is over and twenty-year-old Mike Tyson is the new WBC champion. "I am the heavyweight champion of the world," he tells the television audience, "and I will fight anybody in the world."

The post-Ali era has finally ended.

Boxing is our most controversial American sport, always, it seems, on the brink of being abolished. Its detractors speak of it in contempt as a "so-called 'sport,'" and surely their logic is correct: if "sport" means harmless play, boxing is not a sport; it is certainly not a game. But "sport" can signify a paradigm of life, a reduction of its complexities in terms of a single symbolic action—in this case its competitiveness, the cruelty of its Darwinian enterprise—defined and restrained by any number of rules, regulations, and customs: in which case boxing is probably, as the ex-heavyweight champion George Foreman has said, the sport to which all other sports aspire. It is the quintessential image of human struggle, masculine or otherwise, against not only other people but one's own divided self. Its kinship with Roman gladiatorial combat—in which defeated men usually died—is not historically accurate but poetically relevant. In his classic *Theory of the Leisure Class* (1899), Thorstein Veblen speaks of sport in general as "an expression of the barbarian temperament," and it is a commonplace assumption for many boxers, particularly for young boxers like Mike Tyson, that in the ring they are fighting for their lives. (As Tyson said excitedly, following the Berbick fight, "I refuse to get hurt, I refuse to get knocked down, I refuse to lose—I would have to be killed—carried out of the ring. I would not *be* hurt.")

It should be kept in mind, however, that for all its negative publicity, and the sinister glamour of certain of its excesses, boxing is not our most dangerous sport. It ranks in approximately seventh place, after football, Thoroughbred racing, sports car racing, mountain climbing, et al. (It is far less systematically violent than professional football, for instance, in which, in a single season, hundreds of players are likely to be fined for the willful infraction of rules.) And in a time of sports mania unparalleled in our history, boxing remains the only major sport accessible to what is piously called "underprivileged" youth—the others are Establishment-controlled, sealed off from penetration by men with the backgrounds of Larry Holmes, Hector Camacho, Marvin Hagler, Mike Tyson.

It has always been, in any case, from the days of bare-knuckle prizefighting to the present, the sport that people love to hate. Its image of men pitted against each other in man-to-man warfare is too stark, too extreme, to be assimilated into "civilized" society. "You're fighting, you're not playing the piano, you know," welterweight champion Fritzie Zivic once said.

"Yes, I'm fighting for my life in the ring," Mike Tyson tells me. And, "I love boxing." And, a little later, "Am I a born boxer? No—if I was, I'd be perfect."

In person Mike Tyson exudes the air of an intensely physical being; he is guarded, cautious in his speech, wary of strangers, unfailingly courteous. His intelligence expresses itself elliptically, as if through a mask—though not the death's-head mask of the ring that so intimidates opponents. No doubt the referee's classic admonition, "Protect yourself at all times!" rings in his ears in situations like this—an interview, one of numberless interviews, thrust upon him in the ever-burgeoning phenomenon of Fame. (It is difficult to believe Tyson will ever be fully—narcissistically—comfortable in his celebrity as Muhammad Ali and Sugar Ray Leonard are in theirs.)

Tyson is a young man, a phenomenon, one might

say, of paradoxical qualities: more complex, and more self-analytical, than he has seemed willing, in public, to acknowledge. With his boyish gap-toothed smile and his earnest voice he has disarmed speculation about his future as a precocious titleholder by telling reporters repeatedly that his life is simple: "You wouldn't believe how simple it is. I'm too young to worry about so many things. I let them worry." (Meaning that his professional affairs are handled—and handled, it would seem, with consummate skill—by managers Jim Jacobs and Bill Cayton of Big Fights Inc. and trainer Kevin Rooney.) He acquiesces to media descriptions of himself as a "boy champion"; he speaks, not, it seems, disingenuously, of being a "kid" whose career is a masterwork guided by others—primarily, of course, by the late Cus D'Amato. ("Cus laid the groundwork for Mike's career," Jim Jacobs tells me. "And when I say Cus laid the groundwork, I mean he laid the groundwork—for Mike's entire future career.") The young boxer's relationship to his handlers and to his "family"—an intimate though not blood-related constellation of men and women linked by way of D'Amato—allows him the freedom-within-discipline of the child prodigy in music whose teacher and parents zealously protect him from the outside world. And it is readily clear, speaking with Mike Tyson in the presence of Jim and Loraine Jacobs (my interview was conducted in the Jacobses' apartment in the East Forties, Manhattan, surrounded by boxing memorabilia that includes an entire wall of films and tapes), that he is fully aware of his good fortune; he understands that his emotional-professional situation is close to unique in the notoriously unsentimental world of professional boxing. He is loved by his family and he loves them—it is that simple, and that enviable. If in one sense, like other star athletes of our time, Mike Tyson *is* a child, he is also a fully, even uncannily mature man—a twenty-year-old like no other I have ever encountered.

"I'm happy when I'm fighting. The day of the fight—leading up to it—I'm happy," he says. In his black wool-and-leather sweater, black brushed corduroy trousers, a jewel-studded gold bracelet on his wrist, Mike Tyson looks very different from the man who "destroyed" Trevor Berbick seven days ago in Las Vegas; very different from the iconographic photographs of him that have appeared in various publications, here and abroad. (The Japanese are much taken with Tyson: his photograph has been on the cover not only of sports magazines but of movie and general-interest magazines. How to explain his popularity there, where he has never visited? Tyson smiles and shrugs. "Who knows?") Loraine Jacobs shows me a remarkable photograph of Tyson by Ken Regan of Camera 5 in which, in his boxing trunks, eerily shadowed and outlined by light, Tyson looks like a statue, or a robot—a high-tech fantasy of sheerly masculine threat and aggression. I ask Tyson what he thinks of his image—does it seem strange to him, to be so detached from a "Mike Tyson" who both is and is not himself—and Tyson mur-

murs something vaguely philosophical, like, "What can you do?" Yet it is clear that he too is fascinated by the phenomenon of Tyson; he remarks, a little later, that it would be interesting if he could in some way be in the audience at one of his own fights, where the excitement is. In the ring, in the cynosure of action, the fighter does not experience himself; what appears to the crowd as an emotionally charged performance is coolly calibrated. If Tyson feels fear—which, he acknowledges, he does—he projects his fear onto the opponent, as Cus D'Amato instructed: but little emotion is ever visible on Mike Tyson's own face.

If Tyson is happy in the ring, unlike many boxers who come to dislike and dread their own life's work, it is perhaps because he hasn't been hurt; hasn't been seriously hit; has never met an opponent who was in any sense a match for him. (Do any exist? Right now? Tyson and his circle don't think so.) At the age of twenty he believes himself invulnerable, and who, watching him in action, would deny it? One of the fascinations of this new young titleholder is the air he exudes of "immortality" in the flesh—it is the fascination of a certain kind of innocence.

Asked after the Berbick fight why he is so concerned with establishing a record "that will never, ever be broken," Tyson said, "I want to be immortal! I want to live forever!" He was being funny, of course—he often is, making such pronouncements to the press. But he was also, of course, deadly serious.

Baptized Catholic, he no longer practices the faith; but believes, he says, in God. As for life after death— "When you're dead, that's it." He is quick to acknowledge the extraordinary good fortune, amounting very nearly to the miraculous, that has characterized his life beyond the age of twelve, when, as a particularly unhappy inmate of the Tryon School for Boys in Johnstown, New York, a juvenile detention facility to which he was sent after committing burglaries and robberies in the Brownsville section of Brooklyn, he was brought to the attention of the elderly Cus D'Amato—a man who, judging by the testimony of numerous observers, seems to have had the mystical qualities of a Zen Master. But Cus D'Amato was a boxing trainer par excellence who had already cultivated another juvenile delinquent, Floyd Patterson, into a prodigy-champion heavyweight in the 1950s and had discovered José Torres (world light-heavyweight champion 1965–66 and current head of the New York State Boxing Commission) as an amateur boxer in Puerto Rico. The story is that, having observed the untrained thirteen-year-old Tyson box a few rounds in the gym he ran above the police station in Catskill, New York, D'Amato said to a Tryon School boxing coach: "That's the heavyweight champion of the world. If he wants it, it's his."

This is the stuff of legend, of course. Yet it happens to be true. The precocious criminal-to-be—Tyson's earliest arrests were at the age of ten—is taken up by one of boxing history's greatest trainers; is released into

D'Amato's custody and, two years later, is officially adopted by him; lives, trains, most importantly is nourished, in Catskill, New York, in a fourteen-room house shared by D'Amato and his sister-in-law, Camille Ewald —far from the corrosive atmosphere of the black ghetto, in which, judging from his record, the young Mike Tyson would have been doomed. "Cus was my father but he was more than a father," Tyson says. "You can have a father and what does it mean?—it doesn't really mean anything. Cus was my backbone. . . . He did everything for my best interest. . . . We'd spend all our time together, talk about things that, later on, would come back to me. Like about character, and courage. Like the hero and the coward: that the hero and the coward both feel the same thing, but the hero uses his fear, projects it onto his opponent, while the coward runs. It's the same thing, fear, but it's what you do with it that matters." (Jim Jacobs tells me afterward that much of what Mike says is Cus D'Amato speaking; much of what *he* says is Cus D'Amato speaking.)

Quite apart from his genius as a boxing trainer, D'Amato appears to have been a genius of a spiritual sort, if "genius" is not an inappropriate term in this context. Like a devoted religious elder he instilled in Tyson, and no doubt in others of his young boxer acolytes, qualities of an abstract nature: self-denial, discipline, will, integrity, independence, "character." It was D'Amato's belief that a fighter's character is more important ultimately than his skill: a perception proven, in the ring, only in the most arduous of fights—one thinks of the virtually

Shakespearean struggles of the first Ali/Frazier match, the 1941 Louis/Conn match, the Leonard/Hearns. Most importantly, D'Amato instilled in Tyson that most invaluable and mysterious of gifts, an unwavering faith in himself. "He said I would be the youngest heavyweight in history," marvels Tyson. "And what he said turned out to be true. Cus knew it all along."

Jim Jacobs, D'Amato's devoted friend, a boxing manager of enormous reputation and prestige and the archivist of twenty-six thousand boxing films, says that D'Amato's word regarding Tyson's promise was enough for him: there was no one in the world whose judgment he trusted more than Cus D'Amato's. "When Cus told me that Mike Tyson was going to be heavyweight champion of the world, that's all I had to hear." So internalized is D'Amato's voice, and his instructions regarding the nurturing of the young heavyweight, Jacobs says that when he thinks about what he is doing, he has only to "press a button in my head and I can hear Cus talking to me. What I am doing is precisely and exactly what Cus told me to do."

If Tyson looked upon D'Amato as a father—Tyson's "real" father seems never to have figured in his life—it is evident that D'Amato looked upon Tyson as a son. In an interview for *People* shortly before his death, D'Amato told William Plummer that the boy meant "everything" to him. "If it weren't for him, I probably wouldn't be living today. See, I believe nature's a lot smarter than anybody thinks. During the course of a man's life he develops a lot of pleasures and people he cares about. Then nature takes them away one by one. It's her way of preparing you for death. See, I didn't have the pleasures any longer. My friends were gone, I didn't hear things, I didn't see things clearly, except in memory. . . . So I said I must be getting ready to die. Then Mike came along. The fact that he is here and is doing what he is doing gives me the motivation to stay alive." Though D'Amato died of pneumonia in November 1985, aged seventy-seven, approximately a year before Tyson became the youngest titleholder in heavyweight history, he seems to be alive, still, in Tyson's soul. One man's faith in another can go no further.

Yet it would be imprecise to say that Mike Tyson is D'Amato's creature solely. His initial social shyness masks a quick, restless intelligence; he is not without humor regarding even the vicissitudes of his early life. Of his years as a child criminal—during which time, as the youngest member of a gang, he was frequently entrusted with holding a gun during robberies—he has said, "Please don't think I was really bad. I used to rob and steal but other guys did worse things—they murdered people." At times Tyson lived on the Bedford-Stuyvesant streets, slept in abandoned buildings like a feral child. When he was arrested, aged eleven, and sent to the Tryon School for Boys, no one could have guessed how his life, ironically, had been saved. He was violent, depressed, mute; one of the most intractable of the "incorrigible" boys. When he broke loose it required several adult men to overpower him. One official recalls having seen him dragged away in handcuffs, to be locked in solitary confinement.

Mike Tyson's story reminded me of those legendary tales of abandoned children so particularly cherished by the European imagination—Kasper Hauser of Nürnberg, the "wild boy" of the Aveyron. Such tales appeal to our sense of wonder, mystery, and dread; and to our collective guilt. These children, invariably boys, are "natural" and "wild"; not precisely mute but lacking a language; wholly innocent of the rudiments of human social relations. They are homeless, parentless, nameless, "redeemable" only by way of the devotion of a teacher father—not unlike Tyson's Cus D'Amato. But even love is not enough to save the mysteriously doomed Kasper Hauser, whose story ends as abruptly and as tragically as it begins. And the "wild boy" of the Aveyron loses the freshness of his soul even as he acquires the skills of language and social intercourse.

There is nothing nostalgic, however, about Tyson's feelings for his past. Many of his boyhood friends are in jail or dead; both his parents are deceased; he has a sister and a brother, both older, with whom he appears to be on friendly but not intimate terms. If he returns to his old neighborhood it is as a visitor of conspicuous dimensions: a hero, a "boy champion," a *Sports Illustrated* cover in the flesh. Like Joe Louis, Sugar Ray Robinson, Larry Holmes, et al., Mike Tyson has become a model of success for "ghetto youth," though his personal code of conduct, his remarkably assured sense of himself, owes nothing at all to the ghetto. He is trained, managed, and surrounded, to an unusual degree, by white men, and though he cannot be said to be a white man's black man he is surely not a black man's black man in the style of, for instance, Muhammad Ali (whose visit to Tyson's grammar school in Brooklyn made a powerful impression on him at the age of ten). Indeed, it might be said that Mike Tyson will be the first heavyweight boxer in America to transcend issues of race—a feat laudable or troubling, depending upon one's perspective. (In the light of which, a proposed match between Tyson and the zealously over-promoted "White Hope" candidate Gerry Cooney would have interesting consequences: allegiances are likely not to break down along cursory color lines.)

He will do what he can, Tyson says, to promote blacks, but he does not intend to become involved in politics. He will visit schools, make public appearances, do anti-drug commercials for the FBI and the State of New York. If his replies to questions about black consciousness—its literature, art, history—are rather vague, it should be said that his replies to most questions that deal with culture in a larger sense are vague. Tyson dropped out of Catskill High School in his senior year—"I hated it there"—to concentrate on his amateur boxing in clubs and Golden Gloves competitions under the tutelage of D'Amato; and at this point his formal education, such as it was, seems to have ended. He has virtually no interest in music—"I could live without music." He shrugs aside queries about art, dance, literature; his reading is limited to boxing books and magazines. With Jim Jacobs's library of twenty-six thousand fight films at his disposal he watches old fights with an almost scholarly passion— surely this is unusual, in a practitioner? (Jim Jacobs assures me it is.) For entertainment Tyson watches videos of karate movies, horror movies, occasionally even children's cartoons: no serious dramas, and no movies about the lives of fictionalized boxers. I am spared asking him the obligatory question about the preposterous *Rocky* movies.

It should not be assumed, on the evidence of the above, that Mike Tyson is not intelligent; or that he is intellectually limited. On the contrary, I sensed in him the prodigy's instinctive husbanding of the self: he dares not allow his imagination freedom in areas only peripheral to the cultivation of his talent. Because he is an unusually sensitive person—sensitive to others' feelings, not merely to his own—he does not want to be forced to expend himself in feeling, or in thinking; except of course on his own terms. The awareness of life's tragic ambiguity that serious art provides—the perception, as Henry James describes it in the preface to *What Maisie Knew*, that no themes are so human "as those that reflect for us, out of the confusion of life, the close connection of bliss and bale, of the things that help with the things that hurt, so dangling before us for ever that bright hard medal, of so strange an alloy, one face of which is somebody's right

and ease and the other somebody's pain and wrong"—
would be disastrous for the warrior boxer. When, the
story goes, Alexis Arguello (the great champion of the
featherweight, junior lightweight, and lightweight divisions) met Roberto Durán (the great champion of the
lightweight and welterweight divisions) and proffered his
hand to shake, Durán backed away and screamed, "Get
away! You're crazy! I'm not your friend!" To acknowledge
friendship, let alone brotherhood, always makes it difficult to kill—or to provide for spectators the extraordinary
mimicry of killing that boxing of the quality of Mike
Tyson's involves. Life is real and painful, and steeped in
ambiguity; in the boxing ring there is either/or. Either
you win, or you lose.

The brilliant boxer is an artist, albeit in an art not
readily comprehensible, or palatable, to most observers.
The instruments of his art are his own and his opponent's
bodies. That it is, in a sense, a contemplative art—
contemplated, dreamt-of, for weeks, months, even years
before it is executed—is a proposition important to under-
stand if one is to understand the boxer. ("It's a lonely
sport," Mike Tyson, who is surrounded by people who
love him, says.) Obsession is not greatness but greatness
is obsession, so it is no accident that, in his ambition to
be not only the youngest titleholder in heavyweight history but (I would guess) the greatest titleholder of all
time, Tyson is always, in a spiritual sense, in training.
His admiration for past boxers—Stanley Ketchel, Jack
Dempsey, Henry Armstrong, Kid Chocolate—and, not

least, Roberto Durán, of whom he speaks with genuine awe—is the admiration of the shrewd apprentice for his elders, not necessarily his betters. When I ask Tyson to assess his heavyweight contemporaries, men he will be meeting in the ring in the next few years, he again becomes purposefully vague, saying he doesn't think too much about them: "That would drive me crazy." Pinklon Thomas, Gerry Cooney, Carl Williams, Tyrell Biggs, Bert Cooper—he'd rather change the subject. And this instinct too is correct: the boxer must concentrate upon his opponents one by one, each in turn: in the collective, they cannot be granted existence. I am reminded of a diary entry of Virginia Woolf's to the effect that she does not dare read her serious rivals. "Do I instinctively keep my mind from analysing, which would impair its creativeness? . . . No creative writer can swallow another contemporary. The reception of living work is too coarse and partial if you're doing the same thing yourself" (20 April 1935).

Similarly, Tyson does not want to think overmuch about fatal accidents in the ring. He takes it for granted that *he* will not, indeed cannot, be hurt—"I'm too good for that to happen"; on the subject of an opponent's fate at his hands he is matter-of-fact and pragmatic. He is a boxer, he does his job—throwing punches until his opponent is defeated. If, as in the infamous Griffith-Paret match of 1962, in which Paret, trapped in the ropes, was struck eighteen unanswered blows by Griffith, death does occur, that is no one's fault: it can be said to be an accident. "Each of you takes the same chance, getting into the ring," Tyson says in his soft, considered, alternately slow and hurried voice—one of the voices, perhaps, of Cus D'Amato. "That you might die. It *might* happen."

I ask Tyson what he was thinking when the stricken Berbick tried to get to his feet and he says quickly, "I hoped he wasn't hurt," and adds, "It was a deliberate punch, to the head—a bad intention in a vital area." The anatomical areas Tyson has been taught to strike with his sledgehammer blows include the liver, the kidneys, the heart, and, as in Berbick's case, a certain spot on the temple which, if struck hard enough, will cause a man to drop immediately to the canvas. He will be fully conscious, as Berbick was, but paralyzed. Helpless. Down for the count.

And Tyson is confident that he himself cannot be hurt—in any serious, permanent way?

"That's right. I can't be. I'm too good."

Following the accidental death of one of the Flying Wallendas some years ago, a surviving member of the family of famous aerial-trapeze performers told the press that none of them had any intention of quitting. "All of life," he said, "is just getting through the time between acts."

So too with the fighter who loves to fight; the man whose identity is so closely bound up with the ring that it might be said he has none, publicly speaking, outside it. His creative work is done only in the ring, and only at certain designated times. Taped, it becomes permanent;

it *is* himself—or all that posterity will know of him.

The extraordinary upward trajectory of Mike Tyson's career—twenty-eight professional fights in eighteen months—has been the result of discipline and concentration so fierce as to resemble monastic devotion. Now that he is a titleholder, and a celebrity, and no longer a hungry young contender, Tyson's sense of himself has irrevocably altered; though he has yet to unify the heavyweight title—to do so, he will have to beat "Bonecrusher" Smith for the WBA title and the elusive Michael Spinks for the IBF title—he is already being called, and, in excited moments, calls himself, the heavyweight champion of the world. He has outdistanced his contemporaries—the new young generation of boxers that includes such Olympic Gold Medalists as Tyrell Biggs, Mark Breland, Paul Gonzales, Meldrick Taylor, and Pernell Whittaker; he is the first among them to win not only a title but enormous popular success. "When I was a kid I wanted to be famous—I wanted to be somebody," Mike Tyson says. And: "If someone right now is going to be famous, I'm glad it's me." But fame and the rewards of fame are, in a very real sense, the counterworld of the boxer's training: they represent all that must be repressed in the service of the boxer's real, as opposed to his merely public, career. When boxers retire it is primarily because of the terrible rigors of training, not the risks of defeat, injury, or even death in the ring. (The boxer who is generally credited with having trained hardest is Rocky Marciano, who commonly spent upward of two months preparing for a fight.

And when Marciano decided to retire, undefeated, at the age of thirty-three, it was because the sacrifices of the training camp outweighed the rewards of celebrity: "No kind of money can make me fight again," Marciano said.) The existential experience of the fight itself—spectacular, amplified, recorded in its every minute detail—is not only the culmination of the formidable training period but, in its very flowering, or fruition, it presents the boxer-as-performer to the world. Very likely this physical expenditure of the self (Tyson typically refers to it as "matching my boxing skills against my opponent's"), this bedrock of what's real, casts the remainder of life into a light difficult to assess. Life outside the ring is real enough—yet is it *really* real? Not public display as such but the joy of the body in its straining to the very limits of ingenuity and endurance underlies the motive for such feats of physical prowess as championship boxing or aerial-trapeze work. The performer is rewarded by his performance as an end in itself; he becomes addicted, as who would not, to his very adrenaline. *All of life is just getting through the time between acts.*

Since Mike Tyson is a young man gifted with a highly refined sense of irony, if not a sense of the absurd, it cannot have escaped his attention that, much of the time, in public places like the expensive midtown restaurant in which our party has dinner following the interview, or the reception two weeks later in a private suite in Madison Square Garden before the Witherspoon-Smith elimination match, he is likely to be the only black in at-

tendance. He is likely to be the youngest person in attendance, and the only man not dressed in a suit and tie.
Above all he is likely to be the only person with a gold
tooth and a homemade tattoo ("Mike" on his right bicep);
and the only person who, not many years before, was so
violent and uncontrollable ("I went berserk sometimes")
he had to be forcibly restrained. But when I mention
some of this to a fellow guest at the Garden reception the
man looks at me as if I have said something not only bizarre but distasteful. "I doubt that Mike thinks in those
terms," he says. Not even that Tyson *is* the only black in
this gathering of well-to-do white people, an observation
that would appear to be simple fact? But no, I am assured: "Mike Tyson doesn't think in those terms."

Following a brief speech by the gentleman who runs
Madison Square Garden, Tyson is presented with a ceremonial gift: a glass paperweight apple symbolizing New
York City. He is photographed, he smiles genially, expresses his thanks for the paperweight, stands looking at
it, for a moment, with a bemused expression. When, afterward, I ask Tyson how he likes being a celebrity—
since, after all, he wanted to be famous—he says, "It's
okay." Then: "Most of the time these things drive me
crazy." I observe that he has learned to smile very nicely
for photographers, and he responds with a violent parody
of a celebrity smile: a death's-head grimace that is fierce,
funny, self-mocking, inspired.

Four weeks later, still being photographed—this time by photographers for two magazines simultaneously—Tyson is back in training in Catskill, New York, in a third-floor walk-up gym above Catskill Police Headquarters on main Street. The gym is small, well-weathered, romantically shabby; owned and operated by the city of Catskill but leased for $1 a year to the Cus D'Amato Memorial Boxing Club, a nonprofit organization. In the spareness of the gym's equipment as in the sentiment that so clearly accrues to its homeliest features, it is the very antithesis of today's high-tech high-gloss athletic clubs. It contains only a single ring and a few punching bags; its ceiling is high and blistered, its lights antiquated. Its peeling walls are covered with newspaper clippings, announcements of the Catskill Boxing Club, photographs and posters of great champions (Louis, Walcott, Charles, Marciano, Patterson, et al.), reproductions of magazine covers. Mike Tyson's entire career is recorded here, in miniature, and, beneath the legend WE MOURN HIS PASSING, there are numerous clippings and photographs pertaining to the late Cus D'Amato, who once presided over the Boxing Club. Tyson prefers this gym to any other, naturally: it was here he began training, aged thirteen, and here that D'Amato's spirit still resounds. The gym is as indelibly imprinted in Tyson's imagination as any place on earth, and one must suppose that his prodigious youthful success has consecrated it in turn.

No athletes train more rigorously than boxers, and no present-day boxer is more serious about his training than Mike Tyson. Indeed, for the first eighteen months of his career he seems to have kept in condition more or less as the legendary Harry Greb did—by fighting virtually all the time. Today Tyson has done his morning roadwork— "three to five miles; I like it then 'cause I'm alone"—and is now going through the exercises that constitute "preliminary" training. (In Las Vegas he will work with at least five sparring partners. As Jim Jacobs explains, the sparring partners need time to recover.) Dressed in a black leotard and blowsy white trunks he moves from "work" station to station, closely attended by his trainer, Rooney, whom he clearly respects, and for whom he feels a good deal of affection, perhaps, at least in part, because Rooney is himself a D'Amato protégé—a welterweight who once boxed on the U.S. Boxing Team—and even shared one or two cards with Tyson, when he was already Tyson's trainer.

The drills are fierce and demand more concentration, strength, and sheer physical endurance than any fight Tyson has yet fought. Rooney has set a timer made up of two bulbs, red and green, to monitor each drill, the red telling Tyson to pause, the latter to resume. First he jumps rope, as if in a kind of trance, the rope moving too swiftly to be seen; the spectacle of a man of Tyson's build, so light on his feet, so seemingly *weightless,* has a preternatural quality. Next the heavy bag: Rooney wraps his hands with white tape, Tyson puts on gloves, pushes the bag with his left, then pummels it with combinations as it swings back to him. Rooney stands close and after each flurry the two confer, even as the heavy bag still swings treacherously in and around them. As he launches his hooks Tyson leaps from point to laterial point with extraordinary agility—as if his upper body remains stationary while his lower body moves in sharp angles out of which solidly anchored punches are shot. These are blows of such daunting power it is difficult to comprehend how they could be absorbed by any human being . . . any fellow creature of flesh, bone, and blood.

Rooney is game to try, at least for a while, wearing padded mitts over his hands and forearms; then they move on to the "slip" bag, where Tyson bobs and weaves, eluding his invisible opponent's best-aimed blows to the head. Last, the speed bag. In the blurred and confusing action of a fight it is not so readily clear, as it is in the gym, that Tyson's relative shortness (he is considered a "little" heavyweight) is really to his advantage. Most of his opponents are taller than he, if not invariably heavier, so that they are obliged to punch at a downward angle, utilizing only their shoulder and arm muscles; while Tyson can punch upward, utilizing not only his shoulder and arm muscles but his leg muscles as well—and these muscles are massive. By crouching, he can make himself shorter, and yet more elusive. (As Jim Jacobs has explained, "People speak of a 'height advantage' when what they're really referring to is a 'height disadvantage.' If a boxer is good, and shorter than his opponent, the advantage is his, and not his opponent's. The same thing holds true with the fallacy of the 'reach advantage'—a boxer has a 'reach advantage' only if he is superior to his opponent.") But the strangest, most dazzling thing about Tyson's boxing style is really his speed: his incredible speed. How, one wonders, can he do it? Weighing what he does, and built as he is? And will he be able to keep it up, in the years to come?

"Eat, sleep, and train," says Kevin Rooney. "Mike loves to train."

But: "I'm tired," Tyson says several times, in a soft, nearly inaudible voice. (He is still being photographed.) In his black leotard, towel in hand, he is literally drenched in sweat; exuding sweat like tears. One can see how much easier fighting has been for him than the regimen Rooney has devised—so many of Tyson's fights have lasted less than five minutes, against opponents lacking the skill to so much as raise a welt on his face, or cause him to breathe hard. And this training session is only the beginning—on February 3 he leaves for Las Vegas and four weeks of "intensive" training.

He showers, dresses, reappears in jeans, a white tuniclike jacket, stylish tweed cap, brilliantly white Gucci sports shoes—surely the only shoes of their kind in Catskill, New York? When we're photographed together in the corner of the ring he complains in my ear of the hours he has endured that day alone, facing cameras: "You can't believe it! On and on!" Fame's best-kept secret—its soul-numbing boredom—has begun to impress itself upon Mike Tyson.

Catskill, New York, is a small town of less than six

thousand inhabitants. Its well-kept wood-frame houses
have that prewar American look so immediately appealing
to some of us—the very architecture of nostalgia. Like
Main Street, with its Newberry's Five-and-Dime, Joe's
Food Market, Purina Chows, the Town of Catskill town
hall a storefront facing the police station, and the village
offices—clerk, treasurer, tax collector—in the same
building as the Catskill Boxing Club. Parking here is five
cents an hour.

Mike Tyson lives two or three miles away, in one of
the largest and most attractive houses in town, the home
of Mrs. Camille Ewald, Cus D'Amato's sister-in-law. The
house is at the end of an unpaved, seemingly private
road, immaculately kept outside and in, yet comfortable—"I've lived here for seven years now," Tyson
says proudly. He leads me through a kitchen and through
a parlor room gleaming with trophies he doesn't acknowledge and we sit at one end of an immense living room
while, from varying distances, a photographer (from
Japan) continues to take candid shots of him he doesn't
acknowledge either.

Life in Catskill is quiet and nourishingly routine: up
at 6 A.M., to bed at 9 P.M. Daily workouts at the gym
with Rooney; a diet of meat, vegetables, pasta, fruit
juice—never any alcohol or caffeine; a modicum, in this
semirural environment, of monastic calm. But there are
numerous distractions: last week Tyson addressed a junior high school in New York City, under the auspices of
the Drug Enforcement Agency, and tomorrow he is due to

fly to Jamaica for a boxing banquet at which, however improbably, Don King is going to be given a humanitarian award—"But I'm not going; I'm too tired." He speaks soberly of the responsibility of celebrity; the fact that fame requires, of its conscientious recipients, a degree of civic servitude. The awareness weighs upon him almost visibly.

With equal sobriety, and a mysterious conviction, Tyson goes on to say that friends, certain friends—"some of them the ones you like best"—can't be relied upon. "They want to be your friend, or say they do, then the least thing that goes wrong—" He makes a dismissive gesture. "They're gone." I suggest that this can't be the case with people he has known a long time, before he became famous, like Jim and Loraine Jacobs, and Tyson's face brightens. The Jacobses will always be his friends, he agrees. "No matter if I lost every fight from now on, if I was knocked down, knocked out—they'd always be my friends. That's right." He seems momentarily cheered.

Tyson's prize possession in Catskill is a young female dog of an exquisite Chinese breed, Shar-Pei, with an appealingly ugly pug face, rippling creases of flesh on its back, a body wildly animated by affection. He'd always wanted one of these dogs, Tyson says, but hadn't been able to afford it until now. "In China they were bred to hunt wild boars—that's why they have those wrinkles on their backs," he explains. "So when the boar bit into them they could twist around to keep on attacking." As Tyson speaks fondly of this uniquely evolved creature I am reminded of Tyson's own ring strategy—his agility at slipping an opponent's blows, ducking or leaning far to one side, then returning with perfect leverage and timing to counterpunch, often with his devastating right upper-cut. The "little" warrior dramatically overcoming the larger.... He loves this dog, he says. For the first time today he looks genuinely happy.

On our way out of the house, Tyson shows me the dining room in which he ate so many meals with Cus D'Amato. The room is handsomely furnished, flooded with sunshine on this clear winter day. "Cus sat here," Tyson says, indicating the head of the table, "—and I sat here. By his side."

When Santayana said that another world to live in is what we mean by religion, he could hardly have foreseen how his remark might apply to the sports mania of our time; to the extraordinary passion, amounting very nearly to religious fervor and ecstasy, millions of Americans commonly experience in regard to sport. For these people —the majority of them men—sports has become the "other world," preempting, at times, their interest in "this" world: their own lives, work, families, official religions.

Set beside the media-promoted athletes of our time and the iconography of their success, the average man knows himself merely average. In a fiercely competitive sport like boxing, whose pyramid may appear democrati-cally broad at the base but is brutally minuscule at the top, to be even less than great is to fail. A champion boxer, hit by an opponent and hit hard, may realize the total collapse of his career in less time than it takes to read this sentence. Boxing is not to be seized as a metaphor for life, but its swift and sometimes irremediable reversals of fortune starkly parallel those of life, and the blow we never saw coming—invariably, in the ring, the knockout blow—is the one that decides our fate. Boxing's dark fascination is as much with failure, and the courage to forbear failure, as it is with triumph. Two men climb into a ring from which, in symbolic terms, only one climbs out.

After the Berbick fight Tyson told reporters he'd wanted to break Berbick's eardrum. "I try to catch my opponent on the tip of the nose," he was quoted after his February 1986 fight with the hapless Jesse Ferguson, whose nose was broken in the match, "because I want to punch the bone into the brain." Tyson's language is as direct and brutal as his ring style, yet, as more than one observer has noted, strangely disarming—there is no air of menace, or sadism, or boastfulness in what he says: only the truth. For these reasons Mike Tyson demonstrates more forcefully than most boxers the paradox at the heart of this controversial sport. That he is "soft-spoken," "courteous," "sensitive," clearly thoughtful, intelligent, introspective; yet at the same time—or nearly the same time—he is a "killer" in the ring. That he is one of the most warmly affectionate persons, yet at the same time—or nearly—a machine for hitting "sledgehammer" blows. How is it possible? one asks. And why? Boxing makes graphically clear the somber fact that the same individual can be thoroughly "civilized" and "barbaric" depending upon the context of his performance. "I'm a boxer," Tyson says. "I'm a warrior. Doing my job." Murder, a legal offense, cannot occur in the ring. Any opponent who agrees to fight a man of Tyson's unique powers must know what he is doing—and, as Tyson believes, each boxer takes the same chance: matching his skills against those of his opponent.

The fictive text against which boxing is enacted has to do with the protection of human life; the sacramental vision of life. *Thou shalt not kill* (or maim, wound, cause to suffer injury) and *Do unto others as you would have them do unto you* are the implicit injunctions against which the spectacle unfolds and out of which its energies arise. The injunctions are, for the duration of the "game," denied, or repressed, or exploited. Far from being primitive, boxing is perhaps the most highly regulated and ritualistic of sports, so qualified by rules, customs, and unspoken traditions that it stands in a unique, albeit teasing, relationship to the extremes of human emotion: rage, despair, terror, cruelty, ecstasy. It is an art, as I've suggested, in which the human body itself is the instrument; its relationship to unmediated violence is that of a musical composition to mere noise. There may be a family kinship between Bach and aleatory "music," but the kinship is hardly the most significant thing about either.

But what, one wonders, is the purpose of so extreme an art?—can it have a purpose? Why do some men give themselves to it so totally, while others, as spectators, stare in rapt fascination—and pay so much money for the privilege of doing so?

Wallace Stevens's insight that the death of Satan was a tragedy for the imagination has no validity in terms of the curious aesthetic phenomenon that is professional boxing. In the boxing ring, elevated, harshly spotlighted, men are pitted against each other in one-on-one mirror-like combat in order to release energies in themselves and in their audience that are demonic by the standards of ordinary—or do I mean noncombative?—life. The triumphant boxer is Satan transmogrified as Christ, as one senses sitting amid a delirium-swept crowd like the one that cheered Mike Tyson on to victory. Yet, even before Tyson began to fight, even before he entered the ring, the crowd was fixed upon him emotionally. (As the crowd was fixed, more evenly, upon Marvin Hagler and Thomas Hearns in their April 1985 match, shrieking as soon as the men appeared and scarcely stopping until the fight itself was stopped after eight very long minutes. Ecstasy precedes stimulus and may, indeed, help bring it into being.) For many, Mike Tyson has become the latest in a lineage of athletic heroes—a bearer of inchoate, indescribable emotion—a savior, of sorts, covered in sweat and ready for war. But then most saviors, sacred or secular, are qualified by a thoughtful "of sorts." In any case, it's Tyson's turn. A terrible beauty is born.

Other than boxing, everything is so boring.
—*MIKE TYSON*

as Vegas, Nevada. March 7, 1987. In a ring still
stained with blood from the desperately fought
heavyweight match that preceded it, Mike Tyson, World
Boxing Council champion, at twenty the youngest heavyweight titleholder in boxing history, brings the fight for
unification of the title to James "Bonecrusher" Smith,
World Boxing Association champion, at thirty-three an
aging athlete, and, yet more telling, the only heavyweight
titleholder in boxing history to have graduated from
college—but Smith will have none of it. He clinches, he
backs away, he walks away, he clinches again, hugging
his frustrated and increasingly infuriated opponent like a
drowning man hugging something—anything—that floats.
Referee Mills Lane calls "Break!" repeatedly during the
twelve long rounds of this very long fight but Smith seems
not to hear; or, hearing, will not obey. For the most part
his expression is blank, with the blankness of fear, a
stark unmitigated fear without shame, yet shameful to witness. "Fight!" the crowd shouts. "Do something!" In the

ringside seats close by me Smith's fellow boxers Trevor
Berbick (former WBC heavyweight champion) and Edwin
Rosario (WBA lightweight champion) are particularly vocal, as if in an agony of professional discomfort. For it
seems that the superbly conditioned Smith, who had performed so dramatically only three months ago in Madison
Square Garden, knocking out Tim Witherspoon in the
first round of his WBA title defense, is now, suddenly,
not a boxer: though in that elevated and garishly spotlighted ring with another man, contracted for $1 million
to fight him, performing in front of a crowd of some
13,600 people in the Hilton's newly erected outdoor stadium, and how many millions of television viewers, he
cannot or will not fight. His instinct is merely to survive
—to get through twelve rounds with no injuries more serious than a bleeding left eye and a bad swelling on the
right side of his face; and to go back, professionally disgraced, to his wife, family, and plans for the future ("Being a champion opens lots of doors—I'd like to get a real
estate license, maybe sell insurance") in Magnolia, North
Carolina.

Berbick writhes in the folding chair beside me, mut-
tering, laughing, derisive, very nearly as frustrated as
Mike Tyson, and clearly resentful—after all, he is the
man who fought Tyson here last November, and so spectacularly (and humiliatingly) lost to him, in the third minute of the second round of that fight. He too had tried to
clinch with Tyson, had gripped the young man's arms and
gloves in an effort to hold him back, slow him down, frus-

trate him, but Berbick had also fought him, or made a game attempt—"I wanted to prove my manhood," he said afterward, ruefully, "that was my mistake." In this match Smith's manhood is not evidently an issue. He has no "machismo" to display or defend; if he is a boxer it must be by default. Minute follows minute, round follows grinding round, as Tyson tries to get inside to throw the rapid-fire combinations for which he is famous, and Smith falls upon him and hugs him, clumsily, defiantly, desperately. Mills Lane, exasperated, penalizes Smith by deducting points from him after rounds two and eight. ("I could have deducted a point from him after each round," he said afterward, "but you don't like to do that in a title fight.") The 6-foot-4-inch 233-pound Smith is a zombie tonight, a parody of a boxer, so resistant to boxing's visible and invisible rules, that complex of mores that make boxing at once the most primitive and the most sophisticated of contact sports, it is fascinating to watch him—to a degree.

"I wasn't prepared for how strong Tyson is, how fast," Smith will say after the fight. "Tyson has a devastating left hook." And, defensively: "I did the best I could." Of current heavyweights Smith has invariably been the most erratic in performance, the most unpredictable—capable, under pressure, of boxing well, yet strangely and unprofessionally susceptible to vagaries of mood. Perhaps because he has no real vocation as a boxer—and no more instinct for fighting than one might expect from a man with a B.A. in business administration (from Shaw College, North Carolina)—he is easily demoralized in the ring, allowing childlike expressions of triumph, hurt, bewilderment, and acute unhappiness to show on his face, as boxers so rarely do; he boxes as an intelligent man might box whose intelligence is his only weapon in an action in which "intelligence" must be subordinated to something more fundamental. He draws upon no deeper reserves of self—no energy, imagination, emotion—beyond those of consciousness.

As for Tyson: unlike Dempsey, Marciano, and Frazier, those famously aggressive fighters to whom he is often compared, Tyson is not a reckless boxer; he is not willing, as so many boxer-fighters are, to take four or five punches in order to throw a punch of his own. His training is defensive and cautious—hence the peek-a-boo stance, a Cus D'Amato signature: for is not boxing primarily the art of self-defense? of hitting your man, and scoring points, without being hit in return? For two years, which must have been very long years, D'Amato trained Tyson to bob, weave, slip punches from sparring partners without throwing a single punch in response—a conditioning that has made Tyson an anomaly in the ring. His reputation is for power, speed, and aggression, but his defensive skills are as remarkable, if less dramatic. Confronted with an opponent like "Bonecrusher" Smith, who violates the decorum of the ring by not fighting, Tyson is at a loss; he hits his man after the bell, in an adolescent display of frustration; he exchanges insults with him during the fight, makes jeering faces; pushes, shoves, laces the cut over Smith's eye during a clinch; betrays those remnants of his Brooklyn street-fighting days (Tyson, as a child of ten, was one of the youngest members of a notorious gang called the Jolly Stompers) his training as a boxer should have overcome. In short, his inexperience shows.

So the pattern of the fight is immediately established: in the entire twelve rounds virtually nothing will happen that does not happen in the first thirty seconds of the first round. The spectator is gripped by stasis itself, by the perversity of the expectation that, against all expectation, something will happen. If this is theater, and boxing is always theater, we are in the slyly teasing antiworlds of Jarry, Ionesco, Beckett; the aesthetics is that of fanatic tedium, as in John Cage and Andy Warhol. While my press colleagues to a man will report the match boring —"Two interior decorators could have done each other more damage" *(Los Angeles Times)*—I find it uniquely tense, and exhausting; not unlike the first Spinks/Holmes fight in which the frustrated Holmes carried his right glove for round after round, a talismanic club waiting to be swung. Poor Holmes! Poor Lear! This is the very poetry of masculine frustration—the failure of psychic closure. Such fights end, and are funny, in retrospect; but are never resolved.

Tyson's predicament vis-à-vis "Bonecrusher" Smith brings to mind Jack Dempsey, similarly frustrated in his matches with Tunney, shouting at his retreating opponent, "Come on and fight!" But, for all his renown, Dempsey was not a strategic boxer of the sort Tyson has been meticulously trained to be; his ring style was virtually nonstop offense with very little defense, which means that he was willing to take punches in the hope of throwing his own. Outboxed by the more cautious and more intelligent Tunney, he eventually lost both fights. In the Tyson/Smith match there is no question that Tyson is the superior boxer; he will win every round unanimously in what is in fact one of the easiest fights of his two-year career as a professional. But this is hardly the dramatic public performance he'd hoped to give, and the fight's promoters had hoped to present. No knockout—none of the dazzling combinations of blows for which he is known; very little of what D'Amato taught his protégés was the boxer's primary responsibility to his audience: to entertain. Winning too can be a kind of failure.

The fight recalls several previous fights of Tyson's with opponents who, out of fear or cunning, or both, refused to fight him; yet more worrisomely it recalls Joe Louis's predicament as heavyweight champion in those years when, after having cleared the heavyweight division of all serious contenders, he was reduced to fighting mere opponents—"Bums-of-the-Month" as the press derisively called them. Worse, Louis's reputation as a puncher, a machine for hitting, so intimidated opponents that they were frightened to enter the ring with him. ("Enter the ring? My man had to be helped down the aisle," one manager is said to have said.) For a sport routinely attacked for its brutality boxing has had its share of historically shameful episodes: Louis's title defense against a long-forgotten challenger named Pastor, whom he chased for ten dreary rounds of running and clutching, running and clutching, is invariably cited. While Rocky Marciano/Jersey Joe Walcott I (September 1952) was notable for both fighters' courage—this was the fight that gave Marciano the heavyweight title—the rematch eight months later ended with the first punch thrown by Marciano: Walcott sat on the canvas and made no effort to get up as he was counted out. ("After twenty-three years as a professional fighter, the former champion went out in a total disgrace that no excuses can relieve"—Red Smith, a former admirer of Walcott.) Both Muhammad Ali/Sonny Liston title matches were memorable for Liston's surprising behavior: in the first, in which Liston was defending his title, he refused to continue fighting after the sixth round, claiming a shoulder injury; in the second, he went down with mysterious alacrity at one minute forty-eight seconds of the first round, struck by a devastating, if invisible, blow to the head. (This defeat disgraced Liston and effectively ended his career: he was never to be offered another championship fight. Even the circumstances of his death some years later at the age of thirty-eight were suspicious.) There was Dempsey's notorious fight with Tommy Gibbons in Shelby, Montana, in 1923, which made money for Dempsey and his promoter, Kearns, while nearly bankrupting the town; there was the bizarre "Slapsie" Maxey Rosenbloom, world light-heavyweight champion of the early 1930s, a sort of pacifist of boxing, whose strategy was to hit (or slap, gloves open) and run—a boxing style as exciting to watch, it is said, as the growth of tree rings. While no one has ever questioned Marvelous Marvin Hagler's integrity, his defense of his middleweight title against Roberto Durán some years ago left many observers skeptical—the usually aggressive Hagler seemed oddly solicitous of his opponent. But the most scandalous boxing incident of modern times still remains Durán's decision, two minutes and forty-four seconds into the eighth round of his welterweight title defense with Sugar Ray Leonard in 1980, to simply quit the fight—*"No mas¡"* No more! Leonard had been outboxing him, making a fool of him, and Durán had had enough. Machismo punctures easily.

Though most of Mike Tyson's twenty-eight fights have ended with knockouts, often in early rounds, and once (with Joe Frazier's hapless son Marvis) within thirty seconds of the first round, several opponents have slowed him down as "Bonecrusher" Smith has done, and made him appear baffled, thwarted, intermittently clumsy. "Quick" Tillis and Mitch Green come most readily to mind; and, though Tyson eventually knocked him out, in the final round of a ten-round fight, José Ribalta. Perhaps the ugliest fight of Tyson's career was with Jesse Ferguson, who, in a performance anticipating Smith's, held onto him with such desperation after Tyson had broken his nose that even the referee could not free the men. (Ferguson was disqualified and the fight was ruled a TKO for Tyson.) Such performances do not constitute boxing at its finest moments, nor do they presage well for Tyson's future: to be a great champion one must have great opponents.

Incongruity, like vulgarity, is not a concept in Las Vegas. This fantasyland for adults, with its winking neon skyline, its twenty-four-hour clockless casinos, its slots, craps, Keno, roulette, baccarat, blackjack et al., created by fiat when the Nevada legislature passed a law legalizing gambling in 1931, exists as a counterworld to our own. There is no day here—the enormous casinos are pure interiority, like the inside of a skull. Gambling, as François Mauriac once said, is continuous suicide: if suicide, yet continuous. There is no past, no significant future, only an eternal and always optimistic present tense. Vegas is our exemplary American city, a congeries of hotels in the desert, shrines of chance in which, presumably, we are all equal as we are not equal before the law, or God, or one another. One sees in the casinos, especially at the slot machines, those acres and acres of slot machines, men and women of all ages, races, types, degrees of probable or improbable intelligence, as hopefully attentive to their machines as writers and academicians are to their word processors. If one keeps on, faithfully, obsessively, one will surely hit The Jackpot. (You know it's The Jackpot when your machine lights up, a goofy melody ensues, and a flood of coins like a lascivious Greek god comes tumbling into your lap.) The reedy dialects of irony—the habitual tone of the cultural critic in twentieth-century America—are as foreign here as snow, or naturally green grass.

So it is hardly incongruous that boxing matches are held in the Las Vegas Hilton and Caesar's Palace, VIP tickets at $1,000 or more (and the cheapest tickets, at $75, so remote from the ring that attendance at a fight is merely nominal, or symbolic); it is not incongruous that this most physical of sports, like the flipping of cards or the throw of dice, is more brilliantly realized as a gambling opportunity. In the elaborately equipped sports rooms of the big casinos, where television screens monitor various sporting events, sans sound, and betting statistics are constantly being posted, like stock market reports, one can bet on virtually any sport provided it is "professional" and not "amateur." The favorites are naturally baseball, football, basketball, boxing, and, of course, horseracing, the sport that seems to have been invented purely for gambling purposes. In these semidarkened rooms gamblers sit entranced, or comatose, drinks in hand, staring up at the television monitors and the hundreds, or is it thousands, of postings. Red numerals against a black background. A dozen or more television screens in an electronic collage. The upcoming "fight of the century"—Marvelous Marvin Hagler/Sugar Ray Leonard for Hagler's undisputed middleweight title, 6 April 1987 at Caesar's Palace—is the casinos' dream: as of 7 March odds are posted −3.25 Hagler, +2.25 Leonard, with these propositions: (1) the fight does not go twelve rounds; (2) Hagler by KO; (3) Hagler by decision; (4)

Leonard by KO; (5) Leonard by decision. The Mike Tyson /"Bonecrusher" Smith odds are Tyson −7.00, Smith +5.00, which means that you would make a good deal of money betting on Smith, if Smith would only win. Since Tyson's victory is a foregone conclusion the bookmakers offer only one proposition: that the fight does, or does not, go four rounds. (Which accounts for the outburst of ec static cheering, the only cheering of the fight, when the bell rings sounding the end of round four and Smith, bleeding down the left side of his face, freshly admonished by Mills Lane for holding and refusing to break, nonetheless walks to his corner.)

While in the antebellum American South white slaveowners frequently pitted their Negro slaves against each other in fights of spectacular savagery, and made bets on the results, in Las Vegas the descendants of these slaves, and their black kinsmen from the West Indies, Africa, and elsewhere, freely fight one another for purses of gratifying generosity: the highest paid athletes in the world are American boxers, and the highest paying fights are always in Vegas. Marvin Hagler, for instance, earned a minimum of $7.5 million for his April 1985 title defense against Thomas Hearns, who earned $7 million; in April 1987 he is guaranteed a minimum of $11 million against Leonard's $10 million in a fight that boxing promoters anticipate will make more money than any boxing match in history. ("I'm sure there will be $100,000 bets on both fighters," says a casino proprietor, "and we'll be right here to take them.") Mike Tyson will earn a minimum of $1.5 million for his fight with Smith (to Smith's $1 million) and if his spectacular career continues as everyone predicts, he will soon be earning as much as Hagler and Leonard, if not more. Though Tyson lacks Muhammad Ali's inspired narcissism, he is not handicapped by Ali's brash black politics and Ali's penchant for antagonizing whites: for all his reserve, his odd, even eerie combination of shyness and aggression, his is a wonderfully *marketable* image. (See the iconic "Mike Tyson" of billboard and newspaper ads, a metallic man, no twenty-year-old but a robot of planes, angles, inhuman composure: "Iron Mike" Tyson.)

Yet how subdued the real Tyson appeared, following the inglorious fight, and the noisy press conference in a candy-striped tent in a corner of the Hilton's parking lot: one caught glimpses of him that night at the jammed victory party on the thirtieth floor of the hotel, being interviewed, photographed, televised, and, later, being led through the hotel's crowded lobby, surrounded by publicity people, still being televised, wearing his preposterously ornate WBC champion's belt around his waist and his newly acquired WBA belt slung over his shoulder, his expression vague, dim, hooded, very possibly embarrassed ("It was a long, boring fight—twelve rounds"), like one of those captive demigods or doomed kings recorded in Frazer's *Golden Bough*.

What is "taboo" except that aspect of us that lies undefined, and inaccessible to consciousness: the core of impersonality within the carefully nurtured and jealously prized "personality" with which we are identified, by ourselves and others. In his speculative essay *Totem and Taboo* Freud meditated upon the ambivalent nature of taboo: its association with the sacred and consecrated, and with the dangerous, uncanny, forbidden, and unclean. All that one can say with certitude about taboo is that it stands in perennial opposition to the ordinary—to the quotidian. Taboo has to do with the numinous, with the ineffable, with utter indefinable mystery: with something not us. Or so we tell ourselves.

To the boxing aficionado the sport's powerful appeal is rarely exponible. It seems to be rooted in its paradoxical nature—the savagery that so clearly underlies, yet is contained by, its myriad rules, regulations, traditions, and superstitions. It seems to make the quotidian that which is uncanny, dangerous, forbidden, and unclean: it ritualizes violence, primarily male violence, to the degree to which violence becomes an aesthetic principle. In this, men's bodies (or, rather, their highly trained employment of their bodies) are instruments and not mere flesh like our own. That a man as a boxer is an action, and no longer a man, or not significantly a "man," puzzles those of us who feel ourselves fully defined in any of our actions. The romantic principles of Existentialism in its broadest, most vernacular sense have much to do with one's volition and one's will in creating oneself as an ethical being by way of a freely chosen action. Boxing, more than most contemporary American sports, clearly inhabits a dimension of human behavior one might call meta-ethical or meta-existential. There is no evident relationship between the man outside the ring and the man inside the ring—the boxer who is, like Mike Tyson (or Joe Louis, or Rocky Marciano, or any number of other boxers of distinction), "courteous," "soft-spoken," "gentle," in private life, and, in the ring, once the bell has sounded, "brutal," "awesome," "murderous," "devastating," "a young bull"—and the rest. The aim is not to kill one's opponent, for one's opponent is after all one's brother: the aim is to render him temporarily incapacitated, in a simulation of death. "It's unbelievable," Mike Tyson has said of boxing. "It's like a drug; I thrive on it. It's the excitement of the event, and now I need that excitement all the time."

When the boxer enters the ring, ceremonially disrobes, and answers the summons to fight, he ceases being an individual with all that implies of a socially regulated ethical bond with other individuals; he becomes a boxer, which is to say an action. It might be argued that America's fascination with sports—if "fascination" is not too weak a word for such frenzied devotion, weekend after weekend, season after season, in the lives of a majority of men—has to do not only with the power of taboo to violate, or transcend, or render obsolete conventional categories of morality, but with the dark, denied, muted, eclipsed, and wholly unarticulated underside of America's religion of success. Sports is only partly about winning; it is also about losing. Failure, hurt, ignominy, disgrace, physical injury, sometimes even death—these are facts of life, perhaps the very bedrock of lives, which the sports-actor, or athlete, must dramatize in the flesh; and always against his will. Boxing as dream-image, or nightmare, pits self against self, identical twin against twin, as in the womb itself where "dominancy," that most mysterious of human hungers, is first expressed. Its most characteristic moments of ecstasy—the approach to the knockout, the knockout, the aftermath of the knockout, and, by way of television replays, the entire episode retraced in slow motion *as in the privacy of a dream*—are indistinguishable from obscenity, horror. In the words of middleweight Sugar Ray Seales, 1972 Olympic Gold Medalist, a veteran of more than four hundred amateur and professional fights who went blind as a consequence of ring injuries: "I went into the wilderness, and fought the animals there, and when I came back I was blind."

In Clifford Geertz's classic anthropological essay of 1972, "Deep Play: Notes on the Balinese Cockfight," the point is made that, in Bali, the now-illegal cockfighting obsession is wholly male, and masculine: the "cock" is the male organ, as the Balinese freely acknowledge, but it is more than merely that—it is the man, the maleness, codified, individualized, in a context of other individuals: which is to say, society. The cockfight is utterly mindless, bloody, savage, *animal*—and ephemeral: though a Balinese loves his fighting cock, and treats him tenderly, once the cock is dead it is dead, and quickly forgotten. (Sometimes, in a paroxysm of disappointment and rage,

Geertz notes, cock-owners dismember their own cocks after the cocks are killed.) Boxing in the United States is
far more complex a cultural phenomenon than the Balinese cockfight—it has much to do, for example, with im-
migrant succession, and with the ever-shifting tensions of
race—but some of the principles Geertz isolates in the
cockfight are surely operant: men are fascinated by boxing because it suggests that masculinity is measured
solely in terms of other men, and not in terms of women;
and because, in its very real dangers, it is a species of
"deep play" (an action in which stakes are so high that it
is, from a utilitarian standpoint, irrational for men to en-
gage in it at all) that seems to demonstrate the way the
world really is and not the way it is said, or wished, or
promised to be. The boxer is consumed in action, and has
no significant identity beyond action; the fight is a con-
vulsion of a kind, strictly delimited in space (a meticulously squared circle bounded, like an animal pen, by
ropes) and time. (Jack Dempsey, in whose honor the term
"killer instinct" was coined, once remarked that he wasn't
the fighter he might have been, with so many rules and
regulations governing the sport: "You're in there for
three-minute rounds with gloves on and a referee. That's
not real fighting.") The passions it arouses are always in
excess of its "utilitarian" worth since in fact it has none.
As the bloody, repetitious, and ephemeral cockfight is a
Balinese reading of Balinese experience, a story Balinese
men tell themselves about themselves, so too is the American boxing match a reading of American experience, un-

sentimentalized and graphic. Yes, one thinks, you have told us about civilized values; you have schooled us in the virtues, presumably Christian, of turning the other cheek; of meekness as a prerequisite for inheriting the earth— the stratagems (manipulative? *feminine?*) of indirection. But the boxing match suggests otherwise, and it is that reading of life that we prefer. The boxers make visible what is invisible in us, thereby defining us, and themselves, in a single consecrated action. As Rocky Graziano once said, "The fight for survival is the fight."

It's like being in love with a woman. She can
be unfaithful, she can be mean, she can be
cruel, but it doesn't matter. If you love her,
you want her, even though she can do you
all kinds of harm. It's the same with me and
boxing. It can do me all kinds of harm, but

I love it.

—*FLOYD PATTERSON*,

former heavyweight champion of the world

I t is the boxing match with the distinct premise as its
theoretical axis that is likely to be the most profound,
and in our time the boxer whose matches are most consistently fueled by such interior—if rarely articulated—logic
is Mike Tyson, the youngest undisputed world heavyweight champion in history.

The premise underlying Tyson's first title match, for
instance, with World Boxing Council titleholder Trevor
Berbick, which Tyson won in six brilliantly executed minutes, was that a boxer of such extreme youth (Tyson was
twenty at the time, and fighting in a division in which
boxers customarily mature late), who had never fought
any opponent approaching Berbick's quality, could none-

theless impose his will upon the older boxer: thus Tyson was a "challenger" in more than the usual sense of the word, as, for instance, the luckless Marvis Frazier, son of Joe, had been in challenging Larry Holmes for his heavyweight title some years before.

The premise underlying Tyson's second title defense in Atlantic City, on 16 October 1987, was something along these lines: the twenty-six-year-old challenger, Tyrell Biggs, an Olympic Gold Medalist in the superheavyweight division in 1984, deserved to be punished for having enjoyed a smoother and more triumphant career as an amateur than Mike Tyson; and deserved to be punished particularly badly because, in Tyson's words, "He didn't show me any respect." (Tyson said, post-fight, that he could have knocked out Biggs in the third round but chose to knock him out slowly "so that he would remember it for a long time. I wanted to hurt him real bad.") That emotions between the boxers' managers ran high before the match, very nearly to the point of hysteria, did not assuage the situation.

As with the young, pre-champion Dempsey, there is an unsettling air about Tyson, with his impassive death's-head face, his unwavering stare, and his refusal to glamorize himself in the ring—no robe, no socks, only the signature black trunks and shoes—that the violence he unleashes against his opponents is somehow just; that some hurt, some wound, some insult in his past, personal or ancestral, will be redressed in the ring; some mysterious imbalance righted. The single-mindedness of his ring style works to suggest that his grievance has the force of a natural catastrophe. That old trope, "the wrath of God," comes to mind.

Though there were boxing experts who persisted in thinking that Tyrell Biggs, with his "superior" boxing skills, and his height and reach advantage, could manage an upset against Tyson, for most spectators in the Atlantic City Convention Center the fight was a foregone conclusion. (The odds were ten to one in Tyson's favor.) Not which boxer would win but when would Tyson win, and how decisively, was the issue; and how badly after all would Biggs be hurt. Thus, when Biggs entered the ring, dancing, bobbing and weaving, shadow boxing, a singularly graceful figure in a white satin robe to mid-thigh, with built-up shoulders and fancy trim, accompanied by a sinister sort of music with a jungle-sounding beat, amplified but muffled, the vision was both alarming and eerily beautiful: for here was, not the champion's opponent, but the evening's sacrifice to the champion.

It is difficult to suggest to those whose experience of boxing has been limited to television how very different, and dramatically different, the "live" event is. For one thing, the live match is not filtered through the scrim of announcers' voices; it is voiceless, unmediated. Since words do not encompass it or define it one is not distracted by concepts, nor is one likely to know, from second to second, precisely what is happening, because it happens so swiftly, and irrevocably: no slow-motion replays. Announcers, too, develop homey, formulaic ways of talking about boxing; domesticating it, in a sense—as mellow-voiced narrators of African veldt documentaries domesticate the savage "natural" events of the animated food cycle. By naming, by conceptualizing, we reduce the horror of certain intransigent facts of life; by making the unspeakable speakable we bring it into a comfortable apotropaic relationship with us. Or delude ourselves that we have done so.

The live boxing match, however, suggests that such strategies are of no avail, and the more ferocious the fight, the more relentless the stalking of one man by the other, the wearing-down, the out-psyching, the approach to the knockout and the knockout itself, the more spellbinding the event. If refusing to look at the gouging out of Gloucester's eyes in *King Lear* could prevent that action, there would be some logic in refusing to look, but the event does occur, must occur, and by the terms of the contract we must watch. It is our obligation to the victim to witness, not his defeat, but the integrity with which he bears his defeat.

Real courage is required when you lose, Floyd Patterson once said. Winning is easy.

Matches of such spectacular action as Tyson/Berbick and Tyson/Biggs (arguably Tyson's most intelligently fought fight thus far) suggest boxing's kinship with ancient, or not-so-ancient, rites of sacrifice. The trappings of sport, let alone entertainment, simply dissolve away. One is witnessing the oldest story of our species, the battering of one man into submission by another, the triumph

of one which is the loss (the mock death) of the other; but
the significant issue, in boxing at least, is not this battering so much as the victim's accommodation of it, second
after second, round after terrible round.

Like his predecessor Pinklon Thomas, whom Tyson
handily knocked out to retain his World Boxing Association title, Tyrell Biggs was remarkably courageous in
absorbing Tyson's hammerlike blows, those left hooks in
particular, so that the theme of the fight as a drama became Biggs's quixotic, doomed determination in the face
of Tyson's single-minded assault. The fascination lay in
how long Biggs could endure it, or how long his cornermen would allow him to endure it. (What a surprise to afterward see the fight as Home Box Office televised it, and
to hear Sugar Ray Leonard wonder aloud repeatedly why
Biggs had "abandoned" his game plan—as if the helpless
boxer had had any choice in the matter.) Biggs's strategy
of lateral movement, quick jabs, constant motion was
thwarted almost immediately, confronted by Tyson's superior will and strength; his much-publicized jab was
a flicking sort of jab, a stay-away-from-me jab, while
Tyson's newly honed jab was the real thing, a blow (with
which, in the second round, Tyson split open Biggs's lip).
In retrospect the match seemed a mis-match, like so
many of Tyson's thirty-odd matches, but only in retrospect, since at the start—at the very start, at least—Biggs
seemed to have had a chance. It was Tyson's unremitting
pressure, the intensity of his concentration, his will to do
hurt, that must have broken Biggs's spirit even before

his blows began to take their toll, for never in Tyson's career had he seemed so grimly resolute, so fixed upon destruction, and so exhausting to watch. The tiredness that must have seeped into the marrow of Biggs's bones, not to drain away, perhaps, for months, or years, was felt throughout the arena, a counterpoint to the nerved-up exhilaration of Tyson's attack. (Surely he is the oldest twenty-one-year-old on record?) Tyson has said that he doesn't think in the ring but acts intuitively; like his great predecessor Joe Louis, but unlike, for instance, Muhammad Ali, he gives the chilling impression of being a machine for hitting, and in this most rococo of his fights a machine for rapid and repeated extra-legal maneuvers— low blows, using his elbows, hitting after the bell. Never has a fight, in my limited experience at least, been so oppressively *communal* . . . as if we were all trapped inside the ring's foursquare geometry, with no way out except to be knocked through the ropes, as Biggs would be, at last, in the seventh round. And no way to be saved from annihilation except to succumb to it.

The tension generated by a typical Tyson fight— meaning one controlled and dominated by him—must be experienced to be understood. Tyson/Biggs struck its tone of high expectancy even before Tyson entered the arena (robeless, but wearing the three oversized and absurdly ornamental belts that are the warrior-symbols of his three titles) and built steadily, in some quarters very nearly unbearably, to its climax in the seventh round, when the blood-bespattered referee, Tony

Orlando, stopped the fight after the second knockdown without counting over Biggs. Tyson's ring style, pitiless, forward-moving, seemingly invincible, evokes odd behavior in presumably normal people. Do most men identify with Tyson-as-potential-killer? Do most women identify with Tyson's victims? Or is "identification" in terms of the fight, the spectacle, the playing-out-of-action itself? When a great fight occurs—and Tyson has not yet had a great fight, for the reason that he has not yet had a worthy opponent—the spectator experiences something like the mysterious catharsis of which Aristotle wrote, the purging of pity and terror by the exercise of these emotions; the subliminal aftermath of classical tragedy.

These fights do linger in the mind, sometimes obsessively, like nightmare images one can't quite expel, but the actual experience of the fight, in the arena, is a confused, jolting, and sometimes semihysterical one. The reason is primary, or you might say primitive: either Tyson is hitting his man, or he is preparing to hit his man, and if nothing nasty happens within the next few seconds it will not be for Tyson's not trying. (For a man of Tyson's physical build he is extraordinarily fast with his hands, and he hits in combinations.) In the average boxing match, contrary to critics' charges of "barbarism," "brutality," et al., nothing much happens, as boxing aficionados affably accept, but in Tyson fights (with one obvious exception—the 7 March 1987 title fight with "Bonecrusher" Smith) everything can happen, and sometimes does.

Thus individuals in the audience behave oddly, and involuntarily—there was even a scuffle or an actual fight at the rear of the Convention Hall during the third or fourth round of the fight in the ring, not suggested by the television coverage, and a matter of some confused alarm until security guards broke it up. Some women hid their faces, some men emitted not the stylized cries of "Hit him!" or even "Kill him!" but parrotlike shrieks that seemed to be torn from them—perhaps the "womanlike" shrieks Tyson amusingly described coming from Biggs when he was hit. The boxing commissioner for New York State, ex-world lightheavyweight champion José Torres, seemed to forget himself as he shouted out commands to Tyson (who was oblivious to him as to everyone and everything outside the ring) and to Tyson's cornermen (who were too far away to have heard, should they have wished to hear). Torres's violent hand signals and shouted commands—"Six-five!" was one—would have seemed quite mysterious, if not deranged, had one not known that Torres, like Tyson, is a former D'Amato protégé, and had one not guessed that the ex-champion simply could not resist participating in the mesmerizing action. Strangest of all—and discreetly ignored by HBO television cameras—a fight threatened to ensue between Biggs's chief cornerman, the redoubtable Lou Duva, and the fight's promoter, Don King himself, at the immediate conclusion of the match; each man had to be forcibly restrained from rushing at the other. While television audiences watched the triumphant Tyson striding about the

ring, and the dazed Biggs sitting on the canvas, attended
by a physician, most of us were watching fascinated as
the portly, not-young Lou Duva tried to climb through the
ropes to get at Don King at ringside, the two gentlemen
shouting at each other, for reasons only a few insiders
would know: King had wanted the fight stopped immediately after the first knockdown, fearing "slaughter," but
Duva had insisted that the fight continue, no matter the
risk to Biggs. Duva had his way, and the fight continued
a few more seconds, as if to fulfill its premise—Biggs deserved to be hurt, and to be hurt "real bad" by Tyson.

Boxing's spectacle is degrading, no doubt—in the
most primary sense of the word: a de-grading of the self; a
breaking-down, as if one's sensitive nerve-endings were
being worn away. That the losing, failing, staggering
boxer will not quit is very much a part of the degradation
process, for boxing is as much about losing as winning,
about being hurt as doing hurt, and even the most macho
of spectators is roused to sympathy with the boxer who,
though losing, has displayed that "grace" and "courage"
of which, in another context, Hemingway spoke.

When the fight was over people remained for some
minutes in their seats as if spellbound or dazed, like
Biggs; or exhausted—the twenty minutes of action had
seemed rather more like twenty hours. The prospect of
surrendering Mike Tyson's display of *control* to the quotidian *controllessness* of the world seemed daunting, but
we made our way, a crowd of thousands, milling and
surging, headless, directionless—the yellow-clad ushers,

so much in evidence earlier, seemed now to have entirely vanished—through dour dirty passageways with no EXIT signs and into cul-de-sacs of some terror, for what if, we were all thinking, what if there is a fire? a sudden panic? and we stampede one another to death? a fate some might consider only just, since we had all been witnesses to an action of indefensible savagery?—but, by sheer blind groping instinct, a sort of Brownian movement of human molecules, we made our way out to the street, or into underground passageways that led to the swanked-up tackiness of the Trump Plaza, where figured carpets in primary colors jolted the optic nerve and functionless silly mirrored columns blocked pedestrian movement, showing us what we could not have wanted much to see, our own faces. The fight being over, the "real" world floods back, and the powerful appeal of Mike Tyson, as of his great predecessors, is that, in however artificial and delimited a context, a human being, *one of us*, reduced to the essence of physical strength, skill, and ingenuity, has control of his fate—if this control can manifest itself merely in the battering of another human being into absolute submission. This is not all that boxing is, but it is boxing's secret premise: life is hard in the ring, but, there, you only get what you deserve.

THE CRUELEST
SPORT

And if the body does not do fully
as much as the soul?
And if the body were not
the soul, what is the soul?
— WALT WHITMAN,
"I Sing the Body Electric"

A boxer's victory is gained in blood.
—GREEK INSCRIPTION

Professional boxing is the only major American sport whose primary, and often murderous, energies are not coyly deflected by such artifacts as balls and pucks. Though highly ritualized, and as rigidly bound by rules, traditions, and taboos as any religious ceremony, it survives as the most primitive and terrifying of contests: two men, near-naked, fight each other in a brightly lit, elevated space roped in like an animal pen (though the ropes were originally to keep rowdy spectators out); two men climb into the ring from which only one, symbolically, will climb out. (Draws do occur in boxing, but are rare, and unpopular.) Boxing is a stylized mimicry of a fight to the death, yet its mimesis is an uncertain convention, for boxers do sometimes die in the ring, or as a consequence of a bout; their lives are sometimes, perhaps always, shortened by the stress and punishment of their careers (in training camps no less than in official fights). Certainly, as in the melancholy case of Muhammad Ali, the most acclaimed and beloved heavyweight in boxing history, the quality of the boxer's post-retirement life is frequently diminished. For the great majority of boxers, past and present, life in the ring is nasty, brutish, and short—and not even that remunerative.

Yet, for inhabitants of the boxing world, the ideal conclusion of a fight is a knockout, and not a decision; and this, ideally, not the kind in which a man is counted "out" on his feet, still less a TKO ("technical knockout"—from injuries), but a knockout in the least ambiguous sense—one man collapsed and unconscious, the other leaping about the ring with his gloves raised in victory, the very embodiment of adolescent masculine fantasy. Like a tragedy in which no one dies, the fight lacking a classic knockout always seems unresolved, unfulfilled: the strength, courage, ingenuity, and desperation of neither boxer have been adequately measured. Catharsis is but partial, the Aristotelian principle of an action complete in itself has been thwarted. (Recall the fury of young Muhammad Ali at the too-readily-defeated Sonny Liston in their second, notorious title fight, of 1965: instead of going to a neutral corner, Ali stood over his fallen opponent with his fist cocked, screaming, "Get up and fight, sucker!") This is because boxing's mimesis is not that of a mere game, but a powerful analogue of human struggle in the rawest of life-and-death terms. When the analogue is not evoked, as, in most fights, it is not, the action is likely to be unengaging, or dull; "boxing" is an art, but "fighting" is the passion. The delirium of the crowd at one of those matches called "great" must be experienced first-hand to be believed (Frazier-Ali I, 1971, Hagler-Hearns, 1986, for instance); identification with the fighters is so intense, it is as if barriers between egos dissolve, and one is in the presence of a Dionysian rite of cruelty, sacrifice, and redemption. "The nearest thing to death," Ali described it, after his third title match with Joe Frazier, in 1975, which he won when the fight was stopped after the fourteenth round. Or: "This is some way to make a living, isn't it?" as the superlightweight Saoul Mamby said, badly battered after a title fight with the champion Billy Costello, in 1984.

A romance of (expendable) maleness—in which The Fight is honored, and even great champions come, and go.

For these reasons, among others, boxing has long been America's most popularly despised sport: a "so-called" sport, even a "meta-" or an "anti-" sport: a "vicious exploitation of maleness" as prostitution and pornography may be said to be a vicious exploitation of femaleness. It is not, contrary to common supposition, the most dangerous sport (the American Medical Association, arguing for boxing's abolition, acknowledges that it is statistically less dangerous than speedway racing, Thoroughbred racing, downhill skiing, professional football, et al.), but it is the most spectacularly and pointedly cruel sport,

its intention being to stun one's opponent's brain; to affect
the orgasmic communal "knockout" that is the culminating point of the rising action of the ideal fight. The humanitarian argues that boxing's very *intentionality* is obscene, which sets it apart, theoretically at least, from the
purer (i.e., Caucasian) Establishment sports bracketed
above. Boxing is only possible if there is an endless supply of young men hungry to leave their impoverished
ghetto neighborhoods, more than willing to substitute the
putative dangers of the ring for the more evident, possibly
daily, dangers of the street; yet it is rarely advanced as a
means of eradicating boxing, that poverty itself be abolished; that it is the social conditions feeding boxing that
are obscene. The pious hypocrisy of Caucasian moralists
vis-à-vis the sport that has become almost exclusively the
province of black and ethnic minorities has its analogue
in a classic statement of President Bush's, that he is worried by the amount of "filth" flooding America by way of
televised hearings and trials: not that the Clarence
Thomas-Anita Hill hearing and the William Kennedy
Smith rape trial revealed "filth" at the core of certain
male-female relations in our society, but that public air-
ings of such, the very hearings and trials, are the problem. Ban the spectacle, and the obscenity will cease to
exist.

The aesthetics of boxing is in sharp contrast to its
ethics. Abjured by the referee, "Fight a good, clean fight,
boys!" the boys need not ponder why a "good, clean

fight" is, in fact, morally different from any other. Black boxers from the time of Jack Johnson (the first and most flamboyant of the world's black heavyweight champions, 1908–1915) through Joe Louis, Sugar Ray Robinson, Muhammad Ali, Larry Holmes, Sugar Ray Leonard and Mike Tyson have been acutely conscious of themselves as racially *other* from their audiences, whom they must please in one way or another, as black villains, or honorary whites. (After his pulverizing defeat of the "good, humble Negro" Floyd Patterson, in a heavyweight title match of 1962, Sonny Liston gloated in his role as black villain; when he lost so ingloriously to Muhammad Ali, a brash new-style black who drew upon Jack Johnson, Sugar Ray Robinson, and even the campy professional wrestler Gorgeous George for his own public persona, Liston lost his mistique, and his career soon ended.) To see race as a predominant factor in American boxing is inevitable, but the moral issues, as always in this paradoxical sport, are ambiguous. Is there a moral distinction between the spectacle of black slaves in the Old South being forced by their white owners to fight to the death, for purposes of gambling, and the spectacle of contemporary blacks fighting for multi-million-dollar paydays, for TV coverage from Las Vegas and Atlantic City? When, in 1980, in one of the most cynically promoted boxing matches in history, the aging and ailing Muhammad Ali fought the young heavyweight champion Larry Holmes, in an "execution" of a fight that was stopped after ten rounds, did it alleviate the pain, or the shame, that Ali was guaranteed $8 million for the fight? (Of which, with characteristic finesse, promoter Don King cheated him of nearly $1 million.) Ask the boxers.

Boxing today is very different from boxing of the past, which allowed a man to be struck repeatedly while trying to get to his feet (Dempsey-Willard, 1919), or to be knocked down seven times in three wholly one-sided rounds (Patterson-Johansson I, 1959), or so savagely and senselessly struck in the head with countless unanswered blows that he died in a coma ten days later (Griffith-Paret, 1962); the more immediate danger, for any boxer fighting a Don King opponent, is that the fight will be stopped prematurely, by a zealous referee protective of King's investment. As boxing is "reformed," it becomes less satisfying on a deep, unconscious level, more nearly resembling amateur boxing; yet, as boxing remains primitive, brutal, bloody, and dangerous, it seems ever more anachronistic, if not in fact obscene, in a society with pretensions of humanitarianism. Its exemplary figure is that of the warrior, of some mythopoetic time before weapons were invented; the triumph of physical genius, in a technologically advanced world in which the physical counts for very little, set beside intellectual skills. Even in the gritty world of the underclass, who, today, would choose to fight with mere *fists?* Guns abound, death to one's opponents at a safe distance is possible even for children. Mike Tyson's boast, after his defeat of the 12–1 underdog Carl Williams in a heavyweight title defense of 1989, "I want to fight, fight, fight and destruct the world," strikes a poignantly hollow note, even if we knew nothing of subsequent disastrous events in Tyson's life and career.

Consider the boxing trainer's time-honored adage: *They all go if you hit them right*.

These themes are implicit in Thomas Hauser's *Muhammad Ali: His Life and Times* and *The Black Lights: Inside the World of Professional Boxing*; but it is only in the latter work that theoretical, historical, and psychological issues are considered—Hauser sees boxing as "the red light district of professional sports" in which individuals of exceptional talent, courage, and integrity nonetheless prevail. His *Ali* is the heftier and more ambitious of the two, befitting its prodigious subject—the most famous athlete of all time, until recent years the most highly paid athlete of all time. An authorized biography, it would appear to be definitive, and is certainly exhaustive; Hauser spent thousands of hours with his subject, as well as approximately two hundred other people, and was given access to Ali's medical records. The text arranges these testimonies into a chronological history in which (is this New Age biography?) the author's voice alternates with, but rarely comments upon, still less criticizes, what these others have said. Compassionate, intelligent, fairminded, *Muhammad Ali: His Life and Times* might have benefited from further editing and paraphrase. Specific subjects (an imminent fight, financial deals, Ali's marital problems, Ali's health problems, the Nation of Islam, et al.) become lost in a welter of words; frequently, it is difficult to locate dates, even for important fights. And no ring record of Ali in the appendix!—a baffling omission, as if Ali's performance as an athlete were not the primary reason for this book.

As it happens, Hauser's succinct commentary on the Ali phenomenon and his shrewd analysis of the boxing world, including Don King's role in it, in *The Black Lights*, can provide, for the reader of the biography, a kind of companion gloss; the books are helpfully read in tandem. It is a remark of Ali's, in 1967, that gives *The Black Lights* its ominous title:

> *They say when you get hit and hurt bad you see black lights—the black lights of unconsciousness. But I don't know nothing about that. I've had twenty-eight fights and twenty-eight wins. I ain't never been stopped.*

Muhammad Ali, born Cassius Marcellus Clay in Louisville, Kentucky, on January 17, 1942, grandson of a slave, began boxing at the age of twelve, and, by eighteen, had fought one hundred and eight amateur bouts. How is it possible, the young man who, in his twenties, would astonish the world not just with the brilliance of his boxing but the sharpness of his wit, seemed to have been a dull-average student in high school who graduated 376th out of a class of 391; in 1966, his score on a mental aptitude test was an Army I.Q. of 78, well below military qualification. In 1975, Ali confessed to a reporter that he "can't read too good" and had not read ten pages of all the material written about him. I remember the television interview in which, asked what else he might have done with his life, Ali paused, for several seconds, clearly not knowing how to reply. All he'd ever known, he said finally, was boxing.

Mental aptitude tests cannot measure genius except in certain narrow ranges, and the genius of the body, the play of lightning-swift reflexes coupled with unwavering precision and confidence, eludes comprehension. All great boxers posses this genius, which scrupulous training hones, but can never create. "Styles make fights," as Ali's great trainer Angelo Dundee says, and "style" was young Ali's trademark. Yet even after early wins over such veterans as Archie Moore and Henry Cooper, the idiosyncracies of Ali's style aroused skepticism in boxing experts. After winning the Olympic gold medal in 1960, Ali was described by A.J. Leibling as "skittering... like a pebble over water." Everyone could see that this brash young boxer held his hands too low; he leaned away from punches instead of properly slipping them; his jab was light and flicking; he seemed to be perpetually on the brink of disaster. As a seven-to-one underdog in his first title fight with Sonny Liston, the twenty-two-year-old challenger astounded the experts with his performance, which was like none other they had ever seen in the heavyweight division; he so outboxed and demoralized Liston that Liston "quit on his stool" after the sixth round. A new era in boxing had begun, like a new music.

*"Ali rode the crest of a new wave of athletes—
competitors who were both big and fast . . . Ali had a
combination of size and speed that had never been
seen in a fighter before, along with incredible will
and courage. He also brought a new style to boxing.
Jack Dempsey changed fisticuffs from a kind where
fighters fought in a tense defensive style to a wild sensual assault. Ali revolutionized boxing the way black
basketball players have changed basketball today. He
changed what happened in the ring, and elevated it
to a level that was previously unknown."*

(Larry Merchant, quoted in Hauser)

In the context of contemporary boxing—the sport is
in one of its periodic slumps—there is nothing more instructive and rejuvenating than to see again these old,
early fights of Ali's, when, as his happy boast had it, he
floated like a butterfly and stung like a bee and threw
punches faster than opponents could see—like the "mystery" right to the temple of Liston that felled him, in the
first minute of the first round of their rematch. These
early fights, the most brilliant being against Cleveland
Williams, in 1966, predate by a decade the long, grueling, punishing fights of Ali's later career whose cumula-
tive effects hurt Ali so irrevocably, resulting in what doc-
tors call, carefully, his "Parkinsonianism"—to distin-
guish it from "Parkinson's Disease." There is a true visceral shock in observing a heavyweight with the grace,
agility, swiftness of hands and feet, defensive skills and

ring cunning of a middleweight Ray Robinson, or a lightweight Willie Pep!—like all great athletes, Ali has to be seen to be believed.

In a secular, yet pseudo-religious and sentimental nation like the United States, it is quite natural that sports stars emerge as "heroes"—"legends"—"icons." Who else? George Santayana described religion as "another world to live in" and no world is so *other*, so set off from the disorganization and disenchantment of the quotidian than the world, or worlds, of sports. Hauser describes, in considerable detail, the transformation of the birth of Ali out of the unexpectedly stubborn and idealistic will of young Cassius Clay: how, immediately following his first victory over Liston, he declared himself a convert to the Nation of Islam (more popularly known as the Black Muslims) and "no longer a Christian." He repudiated his "slave name" of Cassius Marcellus Clay to become Muhammad Ali. (A name which, incidentally, the *New York Times*, among other censorious white publications, would not honor through the 1960's.) Ali became, virtually overnight, a spokesman for black America as no other athlete, certainly not the purposefully reticent Joe Louis, had ever done—"I don't have to be what you want me to be," he told white, media-dominated America, "I'm free to be what I want to be." Two years later, refusing to be inducted into the army to fight in Vietnam, Ali, beleaguered by reporters, uttered one of the great, incendiary remarks of that era: "Man, I ain't got no quarrel with them Vietcong."

How ingloriously white America responded to Ali, how unashamedly racist and punitive: the government retaliated by overruling a judge who had granted Ali the status of conscientious objector, fined him $10,000 and sentenced him to five years in prison; outrageously, he was stripped of his heavyweight title and deprived of his license to box. Eventually, the U.S. Supreme Court would overturn the conviction, and, as the tide of opinion shifted in the country, in the early 1970's as the Vietnam War wound down, Ali returned triumphantly to boxing again, and regained the heavyweight title not once but twice. Years of exile during which he'd endured the angry self-righteousness of the conservative white press seemed, wonderfully, not to have embittered him. He had become a hero. He had entered myth.

Yet the elegiac title of Angelo Dundee's chapter in Dave Anderson's *In The Corner*—"We Never Saw Muhammad Ali at His Best"—defines the nature of Ali's sacrifice for his principles, and the loss to boxing. When, after the three-and-a-half-year layoff, Ali returned to the ring, he was of course no longer the seemingly invincible boxer he'd been; he'd lost his legs, thus his primary line of defense. Like the maturing writer who learns to replace the incandescent head-on energies of youth with what is called technique, Ali would have to descend into his physical being and experience for the first time the punishment ("the nearest thing to death") this is the lot of the great boxer willing to put himself to the test. As Ali's personal physician at that time, Ferdie Pacheco, said,

> *[Ali] discovered something which was both very good*
> *and very bad. Very bad in that it led to the physical*
> *damage he suffered later in his career; very good in*
> *that it eventually got him back the championship. He*
> *discovered that he could take a punch.*

The secret of Ali's mature success, and the secret of his tragedy: *he could take a punch.*

For the remainder of his twenty-year career, Muhammad Ali took punches, many of the kind that, delivered to a non-boxer, would kill him or her outright—from Joe Frazier in their three exhausting marathon bouts, from George Foreman, from Ken Norton, Leon Spinks, Larry Holmes. Where in his feckless youth Ali was a dazzling figure combining, say, the brashness of Hotspur and the insouciance of Lear's Fool, he became in these dark, brooding, increasingly willed fights the closest analogue boxing contains to Lear himself; or, rather, since there is no great fight without two great boxers, the title matches Ali-Frazier I (which Frazier won by a decision) and Ali-Frazier III (which Ali won, just barely, when Frazier virtually collapsed after the fourteenth round) are boxing's analogues to *King Lear*—ordeals of unfathomable human courage and resilience raised to the level of classic tragedy. These somber and terrifying boxing matches make us weep for their very futility; we seem to be in the presence of human experience too profound to be named—beyond the syntactical strategies and diminishments of language.

The mystic's dark night of the soul, transmogrified as a brutal meditation of the body.

And Ali-Foreman, Zaire, 1974: the occasion of the infamous "rope-a-dope" defense, by which the thirty-two-year-old Ali exhausted his twenty-six-year-old opponent by the inspired method of, simply, and horribly, allowing him to punch himself out on Ali's body and arms. This is a fight of such a magical quality that even to watch it closely is not to see how it was done, its fairy tale reversal in the eighth round executed. (One of Norman Mailer's most impassioned books, *The Fight*, is about this fight; watching a tape of Ali on the ropes enticing, and infuriating, and frustrating, and finally exhausting his opponent by an offense in the guise of a defense, I pondered what sly lessons of masochism Mailer absorbed from being at ringside that day, what deep-imprinted resolve to outwear all adversaries.)

These hard-won victories began irreversible loss: progressive deterioration of Ali's kidneys, hands, reflexes, stamina. By the time of that most depressing of modern-day matches, Ali-Holmes, 1980, when Ali was thirty-eight years old, Ferdie Pacheco had long departed the Ali camp, dismissed for having advised Ali to retire; those who supported Ali's decision to fight, like the bout's promoter Don King, had questionable motives. Judging from Hauser's information, it is a wonder that Ali survived this fight at all: the fight was, in Sylvester Stallone's words, "like watching an autopsy on a man who's still alive." (In *The Black Lights*, Hauser describes the bedlam that followed this vicious fight at Caesar's Palace, Las Vegas, where gamblers plunged in an orgy of gambling, as in a frenzy of feeding, or copulation: "Ali and Holmes had done their job.") Incredibly, Ali was allowed to fight once more, with Trevor Berbick, in December 1981, before retiring permanently.

Hauser's portrait of Ali is compassionate and unjudging: is the man to be blamed for having been addicted to his body's own adrenaline, or are others to be blamed for indulging him—and exploiting him? The brash rap-style egoism of young Cassius Clay underwent a considerable transformation during Ali's long public career, yet strikes us, perhaps, as altered only in tone: "Boxing was just to introduce me to the world," Ali has told his biographer. Mystically involved in the Nation of Islam, Ali sincerely believes himself an international emissary for peace, love, and understanding (he who once wreaked such violence upon his opponents!); and who is to presume to feel sorry for one who will not feel sorry for himself?

The Black Lights: Inside the World of Professional Boxing describes a small, self-contained arc—a few years in the career of a boxer named Billy Costello, at one time a superlightweight titleholder from Kingston, New York. Like *Muhammad Ali*, it is a sympathetic study of its primary subject, Costello, his manager Mike Jones, and their families and associates; yet, in the interstices of a compelling narrative taking us through the preparation for a successful title defense of 1984, it illuminates aspects of the boxing world generally unknown to outsiders—the routine and discipline of the boxer in training; the complex role of the fight manager; the exhausting contractual negotiations; the state of this "red-light district"—

> *"Professional boxing is no longer worthy of civilized society. It's run by self-serving crooks, who are called promoters . . . Except for the fighters, you're talking about human scum . . . Professional boxing is utterly immoral. It's not capable of reformation. I now favor the abolition of professional boxing. You'll never clean it up. Mud can never be clean."*
>
> (Howard Cosell, quoted in Hauser)

Like others sympathetic with boxers, who are in fact poorly paid, non-unionized workers with no benefits in a monopolistic business without antitrust control, Hauser argues strongly for a national association to regulate the sport; a federal advisory panel to protect boxers from exploitation. His portrait of Billy Costello allows us to see why a young man will so eagerly risk injuries in the ring, which is perceived as a life-line, and not a place of exploitation; why he will devote himself to the rigors of training in a sport in which, literally, one's entire career can end within a few seconds.

Black Lights ends dramatically, with Costello retaining his title against a thirty-seven-year-old opponent, Saoul Mamby, and with his hope of moving up in weight and making more money. Since its publication in 1986, the book has become a boxing classic; it is wonderfully readable, and, unlike *Ali*, judiciously proportioned. Yet to end the book with this victory is surely misleading, and even, to this reader, perplexing. The "black lights of unconsciousness" will be experienced by Billy Costello shortly, in a bout with a dazzlingly arrogant and idiosyncratic Ali-inspired young boxer named, at that time, "Lightning" Lonnie Smith, who would KO Costello in one of those nightmare scenarios all boxers have, before a hometown audience in Kingston. Following that devastating loss, Costello would fight the aging Alexis Arguello, one of the great lightweights of contemporary times, who would beat him savagely and end his career. To end with a tentative victory and not supply at least a coda to take us to the collapse of Billy Costello's career deprives *Black Lights* of the significance it might have had—for boxing is about failure far more than it is about success. In the words of the battered Saoul Mamby, "I'll miss it. I love boxing. Everything passed too soon."

MUHAMMAD ALI

THE GREATEST

*I was determined to be one nigger that the
white man didn't get.*
—MUHAMMAD ALI, 1970

*Boxing was nothing. It wasn't important at all.
Boxing was just a means to introduce me
to the world.*
—MUHAMMAD ALI, 1983

In the twentieth century, and perhaps most spectacularly in the 1970s, sports has emerged as our dominant American religion. Through the excited scrutiny of the media, our most celebrated athletes acquire mythopoetic status; they are both "larger than life" and often incapacitated for life in the ordinary, private sense. To be a champion, one must only be a consistently better performer than his or her competitors; to be a great champion, like Muhammad Ali, one must transcend the perimeters of sport itself to become a model (in some cases a sacrificial model) for the general populace, image-bearer for an era.

Though he came of age as an extraordinary young boxer in the 1960s, and made his mark as a radical political presence during that decade, it was in the 1970s that Ali achieved greatness. The 1970s, following the inglorious end of the Vietnam War, is our decade of transition; a time of accommodation, healing and reassessment. Who would have thought that Muhammad Ali's defiant repudiation of American foreign policy, in the mid-1960s considered virtually traitorous by some observers, would come to be, in the decade to follow, a widespread and altogether respectable political position? Who would have thought that the lone black athlete, like Ali, once ostracized by the media, would come to be emblematic of the "new" era in which, following Ali's example, athletes like Reggie Jackson (the first major league baseball player to sport a moustache since 1914) could express (or exhibit) themselves in essentially playful, theatrical gestures that had little to do with their utilitarian function as athletes? Who would have thought that such flamboyant, controversial gestures as Ali's penchant for declaiming poetry and the comical "Ali shuffle" would influence a new generation of blacks?—in music, where "rap" soared to prominence, and in the scathingly funny comic routines of performers like Richard Pryor; above all in basketball, where players of the caliber of Michael Jordan combined extraordinary skill, like Ali, with a personal sense of style? (Compare the modest, constrained public personae of Joe Louis, Ezzard Charles, Jackie Robinson of an earlier era in which the black athlete was given to know that his presence was provisional and not a right; his very career was a privilege that might be revoked at any time.) The phenomenon of media attention, and hype, accorded every turn of Ali's career was unlike any that preceded, just as the ever-increasing purses and salaries paid to professional athletes in our time are a consequence of Ali's role in the public consciousness. Perhaps free agentry in sports like baseball and football would have followed in due course, but not so swiftly in the 1970s (leading to the 1974 strike in football, for instance) without Ali's example. Ali is the quintessential "free agent" as his much-maligned predecessor Jack Johnson might have been, except for the overwhelming opposition of that era's white racism. And Ali was the Muslim pioneer through whose unwavering example such athletes as Lew Alcindor/Kareem Abdul-Jabbar were allowed to change their names and present themselves explicitly as members of a distinctly non-Christian and non-traditional religion.

Viewed from the perspective of the new century, the 1970s was a transitional period in which, in a sense, a New Era of sports was born. If the celebrity athlete with his astronomical contract is a permanent fixture of American public life, who but Muhammad Ali, once Cassius Clay of Louisville, Kentucky, was his progenitor?

Among boxing historians and fans it will long be debated whether Ali, or Joe Louis, was the greatest heavyweight boxer in history. (And what of the undefeated Rocky Marciano?) It is beyond debate, however, that Ali as athlete, champion, and cultural icon has acquired a significance beyond sports that no other boxer has attained, nor is likely to attain. (Prior to Ali's ascendency in his fights with Joe Frazier, it was the vengeful, brilliantly triumphant Joe Louis of the Louis-Schmeling fight of June 1938 who most captivated the public's imagination. Having been defeated by Nazi Germany's "master race" athlete in 1936, the twenty-four-year-old Louis returned to knock out Schmeling in 124 seconds in the most famous boxing match in American history.) Muhammad Ali's meteoric rise to prominence as an extraordinarily gifted if idiosyncratic and willful young boxer in the early 1960s, culminating in his unexpected defeat of heavyweight champion Sonny Liston in 1964, happened to coincide with at least three historical developments unique to the era: the first, the enmeshed, expanding entanglement of American intervention in Vietnam which both was, yet was not, a traditional war and which was fracturing American society along lines of class, race, generations, and political and patriotic allegiances; the second, the rise of black separatist movements following (in fact, predating) the assassination of Martin Luther King, Jr., in 1968, and the awareness on the part of militant black leaders that since the civil rights victories of the 1950s, black advancement had been stalled; the third, the intensification of media influence and the growth of what might be called electronic mass marketing of "images" detached from content.

"Styles make fights," Ali's great trainer Angelo Dundee said, in reference to his dazzling young boxer's ring performances, but the insight applies to the mass replication of images generally. Cassius Clay/Muhammad Ali soon revealed himself as a master of a new, radically iconoclastic style in public life. He refused to be self-effacing in the cautious manner of his black predecessors Louis, Ezzard

Charles, Jersey Joe Walcott, and Floyd Patterson; the audacity with which he exulted in his blackness called to mind Jack Johnson, the controversial first black heavyweight champion (1908–1915), whose example black athletes (and their white trainers and managers) did not wish to emulate. (Compare the far more cautious yet perhaps not less difficult route of Jackie Robinson in the preceding decade.) Though complicated by issues of religion and race and "ego," the essential message of Cassius Clay/Muhammad Ali in the late 1960s and early 1970s was simple and defiant: *I don't have to be what you want me to be.*

No other athlete has received quite the press—accusing and adulatory, condemning and praising, seething with hatred and brimming with love—that Ali has had. From the first, as the young Cassius Clay, he seems to have determined that he would not be a passive participant in his image-making, like most athletes, but would define the terms of his public reputation. As sport is both a mirror of human aggression and a highly controlled, "playful" acting-out of that aggression, so the public athlete is a play-figure, at his most conscious and controlled an actor in a theatrical event. Clay/Ali brought to the deadly-serious sport of boxing an unexpected ecstatic joy that had nothing to do with, and may in fact have been contrary to, his political/religious mission. His temperament seems to have been fundamentally childlike; playing the trickster came naturally to him. "My corn, the gimmicks, the acting I do—it'll take a whole lot for another fighter to ever be as popular as Muhammad Ali," he remarked in an interview in 1975.

"The acting begins when I'm working. Before a fight, I'll try to have something funny to say every day and I'll talk ten miles a minute . . . I started fighting in 1954, when I was just twelve, so it's been a long time for me now. But there's always a new fight to look forward to, a new publicity stunt, a new *reason* to fight."

At the same time, Ali is deadly serious about his mission as a member of the Nation of Islam; there is nothing playful or trickster-like about his commitment to the Muslim faith ("Muslims . . . live their religion—*we* ain't hypocrites. We submit entirely to Allah's will").

There has always been something enigmatic about Clay/Ali, a doubleness that suggests a fundamental distinction between public and private worlds. And what a testimony is Ali's career of nearly three decades to the diversity of media attention! In our time, in his sixth decade, long retired from the sport that made him famous and from the adversarial politics that made him notorious, Ali now enjoys a universal beneficence. He has become an "American icon" known through the world; a brand name symbolizing "success." He remains a Muslim but no longer belongs to the Nation of Islam; he no longer makes pronouncements of a political nature. He has become a mega-celebrity divorced, like all such celebrities, from history; a timeless mass-cult contemporary of Elvis Presley and Marilyn Monroe.

Yet of course it was not always like this. There were years following Ali's refusal to be inducted into the U.S. Army, as a member of the Nation of Islam, when he was one of the most despised public figures in America; even, in

State Department terms, a "possible security risk"! Boxing audiences didn't greet him with incantatory chants of "Al-*li!* Al-*li!* Al-*li!*" but with boos. It's rare to encounter an athlete who chooses to be a martyr for a principle; an athlete who has made himself into a figure of racial identity and pride. (It was always the hope, to become in time a stereotypical hope, that the black athlete like Joe Louis and Jackie Robinson would be a "credit to his race." What was not desired was racial confrontation and conflict.) The issue of race was always predominant in Ali's strategy of undermining an opponent's confidence in himself and, ingeniously, though sometimes cruelly, fashioning himself as the "black" boxer against the "white man's" Negro. Floyd Patterson, much admired by white America, was particularly susceptible:

> *I'm going to put him flat on his back*
> *So that he will start acting black.*

(In fact, Ali didn't put Patterson flat on his back, but humiliated him in a protracted, punishing fight.) Even as the brash twenty-two-year-old contender for the heavyweight title, he'd dared mock the champion Sonny Liston as an "ugly old bear"—an "ugly slow bear"—Liston, who'd so demolished Patterson! Years later, in 1975, Ali would relentlessly taunt Joe Frazier with remarks that would have seemed, from a white boxer, racist:

> *Joe Frazier is a gorilla,*
> *And he's gonna fall in Manila!*

Yet worse (or funnier): "Frazier's the only nigger in the world ain't got rhythm." Frazier, too, was fashioned by Ali into the white man's Negro; the boxer whom whites presumably wanted to win, therefore isolated from the community of blacks. Is this bad sportsmanship on Ali's part, a sly sort of racist tweaking of noses; is it Ali at his purposeful worst, or simply a manifestation of the man's enigmatic nature, the trickster-as-athlete?

Race has long been an American taboo. The very word "nigger" strikes the ear as obscene; in using it, particularly in the presence of whites, blacks are playing (or making war) with the degrading, demeaning historical context that has made it an obscene word, in some quarters at least. (In another context, the word can be a sign of affection. But this context isn't available to whites.) Ali, intent upon defining himself as a rebel in a white-dominated society, would make of every public gesture a racial gesture: defiance toward the white Establishment, alliance with the black community. The political issue of serving in Vietnam ("No Vietcong ever called me nigger" was Ali's most pointed defense) would seem to have been secondary to the more pervasive issue of black inequity in America, for which Ali would be spokesman, gadfly, and, if needed, martyr. In his *Playboy* interview of November 1975, Ali is quoted as saying that, following the teachings of the late Elijah Muhammad, founder of the Nation of Islam, he believes that the majority of whites are "devils" and that he anticipates a separation from white America: "When we take maybe ten states, then we'll be free."

By making race so prominent an issue in the late 1960s and early 1970s, Ali provoked a predictably hostile response from the Establishment, including the federal government. Though forbidden to leave the United States, he would be exiled within it; as a black Muslim he would be "separate" from the white majority. Indeed, among public celebrities of the America twentieth century only Charlie Chaplin and Paul Robeson, persecuted by right-wing politicians in the 1950s for their "Communist" principles, are analogous to Ali. The black athletes Jackie Robinson and Arthur Ashe, in their very different ways, Robinson in integrating major league baseball and Ashe in his activist phase in the public cause of AIDS education, acquired a profound cultural significance apart from their sports yet were never controversial figures like Ali. Considering the protracted violence of the 1960s, the assassinations of public figures and frequent killings and beatings of civil rights activists, it seems in retrospect miraculous that Cassius Clay/Muhammad Ali, the self-declared "nigger that the white man didn't get," didn't provoke violence against himself.

Ali rode the crest of a new wave of athletes—competitors who were both big and fast . . . Ali had a combination of size and speed that had never been seen in a fighter before, along with incredible will and courage. He also brought a new style to boxing . . . Jack Dempsey changed fisticuffs from a kind where fighters fought in a tense defensive style to a wild sensual assault. Ali revo-

lutionized boxing the way black basketball players changed basketball today. He changed what happened in the ring, and elevated it to a level that was previously unknown. —LARRY MERCHANT

The extraordinary career of Cassius Clay/Muhammad Ali is one of the longest, most varied and sensational of boxing careers. Like Joe Louis, Sugar Ray Robinson and Archie Moore, among few others in so difficult and dangerous a sport, Ali defended his title numerous times over a period of many years; he won, he lost, he won and he lost; beginning brilliantly in 1960 as an Olympic gold medalist and ending, not so brilliantly, yet courageously, in 1981. What strikes us as remarkable about Ali is that, while as the brash young challenger Cassius Clay he'd been ready to quit his first title fight, with Sonny Liston, in an early round (with the complaint that "something was in his eye"), he would mature to fight fights that were virtually superhuman in their expenditure of physical strength, moral stamina, intelligence and spirit: the long, gruelling, punishing fights with Joe Frazier (which, in turn, Ali lost, and won, and won); and the famous Rope-a-Dope match with then-champion George Foreman in Zaire, in 1974, which restored Ali's title to him. Never has a boxer so clearly sacrificed himself in the finely honed, ceaselessly premeditated practice of his craft as Ali.

This long career might be helpfully divided into three, disproportionate phases: the first, 1960–67, the "Float Like a Butterfly, Sting Like a Bee" Era when Ali's youthful boxing skills were at their zenith; the second, 1971–78, Ali's return after his three-and-a-half-year exile from boxing; and the diminished third, a kind of twilit epilogue ending with Ali's belated retirement at the age of forty. F. Scott Fitzgerald's cryptic remark, "There are no second acts in American lives," would seem to be refuted by the example of Ali; dazzling as he was as a young boxer, he becomes more interesting in his second phase as a boxer no longer young who must rely upon superior intelligence and cunning in the ring, as well as the potentially dangerous ability to "take a punch"; bringing to bear against his hapless opponents some of the psychic warfare we associate with actual warfare. That is, the wish to destroy the opponent's spirit before the body is even touched.

1960–1967. "Float like a butterfly, destroy like a viper" might have been a more accurate metaphor for Cassius Clay/Muhammad Ali in these early fights. Not until the emergence of Mike Tyson at an even younger age in the mid-1980s would a young heavyweight boxer make such an impact upon his sport as this Olympic gold medalist turned pro after 108 amateur bouts. Born Cassius Marcellus Clay in Louisville, Kentucky, on January 17, 1942, grandson of a slave but reared in a comfortable, supportive black middle-class environment, the young Cassius Clay was like no other heavyweight in history: massive, perfectly proportioned, a Nijinsky with lethal fists and a manner both in and out of the ring that might be called inflammatory. By instinct, Clay knew that boxing is, or should be, *entertaining.* Boxing is, or should be, *drama.* From the campy pro wrestler Gorgeous George, he'd learned that people will buy tickets to see a boxer lose as well as to see a boxer win. Calling attention to oneself, cartoon- and comic-book-style, is a way of calling attention to the fight, and to box office revenue. The early disdain of boxing experts for "The Mouth" is certainly understandable in the light of boxing's tradition of reticent champions (like Louis); a boxer should speak with his fists, not his mouth. With adolescent zest, predating the insouciance of black rap music, Cassius Clay repudiated all this.

> *This is the legend of Cassius Clay,*
> *The most beautiful boxer in the world today.*
>
> *He talks a great deal and brags indeedy*
> *Of a muscular punch that's incredibly speedy.*
>
> *The fistic world was dull and weary,*
> *With a champ like Liston things had to be dreary.*
>
> *Then someone with color, someone with dash,*
> *Brought fight fans a-runnin' with cash.*
>
> *This brash young boxer is something to see*
> *And the heavyweight championship is his destiny.*

And much, much more.

Of course, the young boxer's arrogant verbosity and pre-fight antics were more than balanced by his ring discipline and boxing skill. From the first, Clay attracted media attention as much for his style as for his victories. What was unique about Clay in the 1960s? Even after his wins against such highly regarded veterans as Archie Moore and Henry Cooper (whose face Clay savagely bloodied in a bout in England in 1963), the eccentricities of Clay's style aroused skepticism and sometimes alarm in commentators. A. J. Liebling described this bizarre heavyweight as "skittering . . . like a pebble over water." He held his gloves low, as a boxer is trained not to do. He leaned away from his opponent's punches instead of slipping them, as a boxer is trained not to do. He feinted, he clowned, he shrugged his head and shoulders in odd ways, even as he danced in a sort of sidelong way. He performed a "shuffling" movement to distract opponents and entertain spectators. In the words of Garry Wills, Clay "carries his head high and partly exposed so that he can see everything all the time . . . whips his head back just enough to escape a punch without losing sight of his man." In Hugh McIlvanney's prophetic words, the young boxer seemed to see his life as a "strange, ritualistic play" in which his hysterical rantings were required by "the script that goes with his destiny." Norman Mailer wrote extensively and with romantic passion of the young boxer as a "six-foot parrot who keeps screaming at you that he is the center of the stage. 'Come and get me, fool,' he says. 'You can't, 'cause you don't know who I am. You don't know *where* I am. I am human intelligence and you don't even know if I'm good or evil.' " Of the distinctive, idiosyncratic Cassius Clay style, his trainer Angelo Dundee said in an interview:

He wasn't a guy who was led easily. You've got to remember the intricacies of training this kid. You didn't

*train him like the usual fighter. He resented direction,
so I used indirection. I cast the illusion of him doing
something when he wasn't. To get him to do what he
should be doing.*

["We Never Saw Muhammad Ali at His Best"]

What any boxer "should" be doing is winning, and Cassius
Clay was perhaps no more inventive or flamboyant than he
needed to be to rack up victory after victory to ever-
increasing public acclaim.

Consider the first, shocking title fight with Sonny Liston (shocking because the seven-to-one underdog Clay won
so handily and the seemingly unbeatable champion ignominiously quit on his stool after six rounds): the younger
boxer simply out-boxed, out-punched, out-danced, out-
maneuvered and out-psyched his older opponent. What an
upset in boxing history, on February 25, 1964! This fight is
fascinating to watch, like a dramatized collision of two gen-
erations/two eras/two cultures; a fairy tale in which the audacious young hero dethrones the ogre exactly according to
the young hero's predictions.

Yet what controversy followed when Cassius Clay announced that he was changing his debased "slave" name to
"Muhammad Ali"; he'd been converted to the black militant Nation of Islam (more generally known as the Black
Muslims) and was "no longer a Christian." With remarkable composure, the young athlete who'd seemed so adolescent was publicly and courageously re-defining himself as
black. As virtually no other black athlete of great distinc-

tion had done, Ali was repudiating the very white political, social, and economic Establishment that helped create him. As, three years later, he would yet more provocatively define himself as a conscientious objector who refused to be inducted into the U.S. Army to fight in Vietnam, with the punitive result that he would be stripped of his title and license to box in the United States. (Interesting to note that the majority of white publications, including even *The New York Times,* as well as television commentators, refused through the 1960s to acknowledge Ali's new, legal name; as if the former Cassius Clay hadn't the right to change his name to Muhammad Ali—or to any name he chose. It might have been the quixotic hope that if they refused to sanction "Ali" in the media, his allegiance to the Nation of Islam, if not to *blackness* itself, might simply fade away.)

Between February 1964 and his ascension to heavyweight champion and April 1967 when he was forced into an involuntary exile, Ali successfully defended his title nine times. Widespread white disapproval of his new identity didn't discourage boxing fans from attending his spectacular fights. Among these, the May 1965 rematch with Sonny Liston proved even more disappointing and, for Liston, more ignominious, than the first fight: this time Liston quickly went down in the first round and stayed down, felled by what many boxing commentators saw as a "mystery punch" of Ali's that put Liston out of the fight even as an enraged Ali, adrenaline pumping, screamed for him to get up and fight. (Did Liston throw the fight? Did Liston so fear Ali, he couldn't fight? The sight of Liston lolling on the canvas recalls the similarly fallen—and feigning?—Jack Johnson who lost his heavyweight title to the White Hope Jess Willard in 1915 in the twenty-sixth round of their marathon match. Yet Angelo Dundee would claim to have seen the punch, "a good right hand to the temple my guy threw from up on the balls of his feet . . . He was out. He was definitely out.") Liston, believed to be mob-connected, would be found dead in 1970 in Las Vegas, allegedly of a drug overdose, possibly of murder. One of the shabbier and more sordid episodes in America's *noir* sport.

Other title defenses of Ali's, however, were hard-fought and legitimately won by the champion; brilliant displays of boxing to reach their zenith in November 1966 in a match with the veteran Cleveland Williams, as Ali, ever in motion, ever flicking his unerring left jab at his frustrated opponent, moving head and shoulders with the seemingly casual aplomb of a dancer, unleashing the Ali shuffle, knocked Williams down several times with multiple punches before knocking him out in the third round. What deadly grace, what lethal beauty in motion! And what a mystery Ali's quicksilver ring style would have been without slow-motion replays! In great displays of boxing, as in few other sports, the unaided eye is simply inadequate to catch, let alone register and interpret, crucial moves. If there is a single fight of Ali's that best exhibits his "float like a butterfly, sting like a bee" style, it's this fight with Cleveland Williams. And, unlike the great fights to come in the 1970s, this fight is short.

Soon afterward, Ali's early dazzling career would

come to an abrupt end. Increasingly controversial as a result of his public commitment to the Nation of Islam (which was regarded by many whites and some blacks as a black-racist cult), Muhammad Ali drew a maelstrom of censure when, in April 1967, he refused to be inducted into the U.S. Army and, besieged by the media, uttered one of the classic, incendiary remarks of that incendiary epoch: "Man, I ain't got no quarrel with them Vietcong." He would be found guilty of "knowingly and unlawfully refusing induction" in a Federal court in Houston, Texas, and given, by an elderly white judge, the stiffest possible sentence: five years in prison and a $10,000 fine. (Ali's mentor Elijah Muhammad served just three years for urging his followers to resist the World War II draft.) There would be years of appeals, enormous legal bills and continued controversy, but Ali would spend no time in jail. Neither would he be allowed to box in the prime of his fighting life, a melancholy loss acknowledged by Angelo Dundee—"We never saw Muhammad Ali at his best." Not only did boxing commissions refuse to sanction the undefeated heavyweight champion to box, but the State Department, in a repressive tactic bringing to mind the persecutions of Charlie Chaplin and Paul Robeson in the 1950s, revoked Ali's passport so that he couldn't fight abroad.

1971–78. The Return. The Superfights. Then, with fairy-tale logic, as the Vietnam War wound down, a bitter and yet unresolved episode in our history, and the tide of public opinion shifted against the military, the U.S. Supreme Court overthrew Ali's 1967 conviction and he was reinstated as a boxer. Like a rogue elephant exiled to the periphery of his world yet always conscious of, and always uneasily observed by, that world, Ali returned in triumph—almost!—to reclaim his title. In this seven-year period belong Ali's greatest fights, and to say that they were unanticipated is not to disparage the younger boxer but to extol the older. In the intensely fought, physically exhausting fights with Joe Frazier and George Foreman, Muhammad Ali proved himself a great, and not merely a gifted and charmed athlete. After three and a half years of not boxing, though only twenty-nine, Ali was conspicuously slower and knew better than to dance away from his opponent; he would have to compensate for his lost agility with sheerly boxing (and punching) technique; he would have to train to take, and not exclusively give, punishment. That this was a deliberate strategy is important to note. As Ali said in an interview in 1975:

> I don't train like other boxers. For instance, I let my sparring partners try to beat up on me about eighty percent of the time. I go on the defense and take a couple of hits to the head and the body, which is good: You gotta condition your body and brain to take those shots, 'cause you're gonna get hit hard a couple of times in every fight. Meanwhile, I'm not gonna beat up on my sparring partners . . . If I kill myself punching at them, it'll take too much out of me. When you're fightin' as much as I have lately, you're supposed to be boxin' and doin' something every day, but I can't dance and move

every day like I should, because my body won't let me.
So I have to stall my way through.

If this sounds like a recipe for disaster it was also, for Ali, in the short run at least, a recipe for success. Indeed, it is the game-plan for the remainder of Ali's career, the strategy that would win him two of his epic fights with Joe Frazier and the legendary Foreman fight in which, miraculously, or so it seems, the younger, stronger and seemingly more dangerous Foreman would punch himself out on Ali's stubborn body in eight rounds, to relinquish the heavyweight title another time to Ali. As Ali's doctor at that time, Ferdie Pacheco, said:

Ali discovered something which was both very good and
very bad. Very bad in that it led to the physical damage
he suffered later in his career; very good in that it even-
tually got him back the championship. He discovered
that he could take a punch.

And take punches Ali did, for the next six years.

The great, extravagantly publicized matches of this period of Ali's career belong with the great sports events of all time. Frazier-Ali I (1971) (which attracted more viewers than any boxing match in history), Ali-Frazier II (1974), Ali-Frazier III (1975), and Ali-Foreman (1974) would seem to inhabit an archetypal realm of the spirit that transcends most sports events. The perilous, cathartic heights of Greek and Shakespearean tragedy come to mind when we consider these draining fights in which even the winners are irrevocably altered. (After fourteen rounds of the "Thriller in Manila" with Frazier in 1975, Ali, the winner, nonetheless described the experience as "The nearest thing to death.") Not surprisingly, these epic boxing matches excited media interest and drew to Ali's camp numerous commentators, some of them famous in themselves (like George Plimpton, Norman Mailer), who would spend more than a month in Zaire for the Ali-Foreman fight. (See the Academy Award-winning documentary *When We Were Kings,* and Norman Mailer's highly stylized coverage *The Fight.*) Not just Ali's stoical courage as an athlete, but Ali's ingenuity drew such attention. For even the aging Ali was a meta-athlete who conceived of his public appearances as theater, not merely, or wholly sport; Ali was a superb athlete, but he was also a superb actor, exhibiting "Ali" to the acclaim of millions. Watching Ali in what we might call his aging prime, we are reminded of Jean-Paul Sartre's remark *Genius is not a gift, but the way a person invents in desperate circumstances.* There is something of the con-man in Ali, and his game is to make us want to believe in his indestructibility, even as, perhaps, Ali doesn't, or can't, believe in it without qualification himself. Consider the Foreman fight. In *When We Were Kings,* Foreman is repeatedly "dissed"; he is the opponent whom we are invited to scorn, because he is not Ali, our hero. (In a sense, there is room for only one boxer in the ring, if that boxer is Ali. He won't play fair in seeking an audience's attention.) As in a fairy tale of heroes and villains, Foreman, for all his gifts, is the villain. Even as we watch this astonishing fight between an aging Muhammad Ali and a young and vigorous George Foreman, reputedly one of the hardest-hitting heavyweight punchers of all time, we are mystified: how did Ali do it? Granted even his superhuman will, how did his body withstand such repeated, relentless blows? The Rope-a-Dope strategy is the very triumph of purposeful masochism; yet such triumph inevitably carries with it irretrievable loss. (Would Ali have wished to win over Foreman had he been able to anticipate his physical and mental deterioration—his "Parkinsonianism"—of later years?) Wittily titled the "Rumble in the Jungle," as if it were but a cartoon or comic-book event, this fight which returned his title to him surely contributed to Ali's taking into his body the "nearest thing to death."

Following these remarkable fights, Ali would exult in being again "King of the World"—"The Greatest." He had secured his position as the most famous athlete of the 1970s, and perhaps of all time. He had traded his health, it would develop, but such a trade would perhaps have seemed worth it, at the time. Unlike the only undefeated heavyweight champion in history, Rocky Marciano, Ali fought worthy opponents, most of them younger than himself. He would defend his hard-won title several times, against such opponents as Chuck Wepner, Ken Norton (who would break his jaw), Jimmy Young (who would break his eardrum), and Ernie Shavers; unexpectedly, he would lose on points to the young Leon Spinks (with only seven pro fights to his credit) in 1978. Though Ali would beat Spinks in their rematch, and announce his retirement, he would be unable to resist returning to the ring; two years later he would be beaten decisively, and painfully, by his former sparring partner Larry Holmes. By this time Ali was thirty-eight and long past his prime; his career had in effect ended with the 1978 loss to Spinks.

1978–1981. The Twilight Epilogue. Yet like many another former champion (Louis, Ezzard Charles, Ray Robinson, Ray Leonard, Roberto Duran et al.) Muhammad Ali would continue to fight, if not to box with any degree of his former talent. His final match, sanctioned not in the United States but in the Bahamas in crude, unprofessional surroundings (a cowbell was used in place of a defective ring bell) was with a mediocre twenty-eight-year-old Trevor Berbick who easily outscored a slow, heavy, plodding Ali on points. For there is a point at which even the ingenuity of desperation fails. (Berbick would have the distinction in 1986 of being spectacularly floored in the second round of his title defense by boxing's new prodigy, Mike Tyson, who would formally end the "post-Ali era.") As the English sportswriter Hugh McIlvanney noted, "Graceful exits are rare in professional boxing but few great champions have gone out more miserably than Muhammad Ali."

In 1981, this time permanently, Ali would retire with a record of 56 wins, 5 losses. But even in the waning years of his career he would be an emblem of the courage and stoicism of the aging athlete, so much a part of our contemporary scene. (Ironically, it would be Ali's old opponent George Foreman who would return to the ring as a "mature" boxer and captivate, in another era, the attention, and affection, of millions of viewers.)

He who was once the icon-breaker is now an icon.

Interview quotations and other material used in this essay have been drawn from *The Muhammad Ali Reader* edited by Gerald Early (Ecco Press, 1998); *In This Corner: Great Boxing Trainers Talk About Their Art* edited by Dave Anderson (Morrow, 1991); and *McIlvanney on Boxing* by Hugh McIlvanney (Beaufort Books, 1982).

IN THE RING
AND OUT

JACK JOHNSON

It was a scandalous and historic American spectacle yet
it took place in Sydney, Australia. It had the elements of
a folk ballad set to an accelerated Scott Joplin tempo. It
might have been a silent film comedy or a Chaplinesque
farce for its principal actors were a wily black Trickster and
a blustering white racist Hero: heavyweight contender Jack
Johnson versus heavyweight champion Tommy Burns for
the world title in December 1908. Though the arena in
which the boxers fought reverberated with cries of
"coon"—"flash nigger"—"the hatred of twenty thousand
whites for all the negroes in the world," as the *Sydney Bul-
letin* reported, yet the match would prove to be a dazzling
display of the "scientific" boxing skills of the thirty-year-
old Johnson, as agile on his feet and as rapid with his gloves
as any lightweight. The setting for this historic encounter
was Australia and not North America for the long-shunned
Negro contender had had to literally pursue the white
champion to the ends of the earth—to England, Ireland,
France, and at last Australia—in order to shame him into
defending his title. The bloody outcome of the fight,

Johnson's victory over Burns in the fourteenth round, the first time in history that a Negro defeated a white man for the heavyweight title, was an astonishment in sports circles and seems to have provoked racial hysteria on several continents. Immediately, it was interpreted in apocalyptic terms:

> *Is the Caucasian played out? Are the races we have been calling inferior about to demand to us that we must draw the color line in everything if we are to avoid being whipped individually and collectively?*
>
> [*Detroit Free Press*, January 1, 1909]

If as John L. Sullivan famously declared, the heavyweight champion is "the man who can lick any son of a bitch in the world," what did the ascendency of the handsome and stylish "flash nigger" Jack Johnson portend for the white race? Jack London, at that time the most celebrated of American novelists and an ostensibly passionate socialist, covered the fight for the *New York Herald* in the most sensational race-baiting terms, as Geoffrey C. Ward notes in this compelling new biography of Johnson, transforming a sporting event into a "one-sided racial drubbing that cried out for revenge":

> *It had not been a boxing match but an "Armenian massacre" . . . a "hopeless slaughter" in which a playful "giant Ethiopian" had toyed with Burns as if he'd been a "naughty child." It had matched "thunderbolt blows against butterfly flutterings." London was disturbed*

not so much by the new champion's victory—"All hail to Johnson," he wrote; he had undeniably been "best man"—as by the evident glee with which he had imposed his will upon the hapless white man: "A golden smile tells the story, and that golden smile was Johnson's."

Summing up the collective anxiety of his race, the poet Henry Lawson gloomily prophesied:

It was not Burns that was beaten—for a nigger has smacked your face. Take heed—I am tired of writing— but O my people take heed. For the time may be near for the mating of the Black and the White to Breed.

As if to fan the flames of Caucasian sexual anxiety, the new Negro heavyweight champion returned in triumph from Australia with a white woman as his companion, whom he introduced to reporters as his wife. (She wasn't.) Through his high-profile career Johnson would flagrantly consort with white women ranging from prostitutes to comfortably well-off married women; in all, he would marry three. The first, Etta Duryea, who may have left her husband for Johnson, became so socially ostracized that she attempted suicide repeatedly and finally succeeded in killing herself with a revolver. Johnson's other liaisons were equally publicized and turbulent. In the prime of his career as the greatest heavyweight boxer of his time Johnson had the distinction of being denounced by the righteous Negro educator Booker T. Washington for "misrepresenting the colored people of this country" even as he was denounced at a National Governors' Conference by, among vehement others, the North Carolina governor who pleaded for the champion to be lynched: "There is but one punishment, and that must be speedy, when the negro lays his hand upon the person of a white woman." (Since 1900, nearly seven hundred Negroes had been lynched in the United States, for allegedly "sexual" reasons.) In 1913, Johnson had the further distinction of being the catalyst for the introduction of statutes forbidding miscegenation in the legislatures of numerous states; at this time, interracial marriage was officially outlawed in thirty of the forty-six states. (None of the proposed statutes of 1913 passed into law and fifty-four years later, the U.S. Supreme Court declared all such laws unconstitutional.) It would seem that Jack Johnson was simultaneously the most famous and the most notorious Negro of his time, whose negative example shaped the low-profile public careers of his Negro successors through nearly five decades.[1] Only in the 1960s, with the emergence of the yet more intimidating Sonny Liston and the brash, idiosyncratic Cassius Clay/Muhammad Ali, was Johnson vindicated. The massive Liston, hulking and scowling and resistant to all white liberal efforts to appropriate him, was Jack Johnson revived and reconstituted as a blackness ten times black. Ali, as viciously reviled in the 1960s as he is piously revered today, was a youthful admirer of Johnson: " 'I grew to love the Jack Johnson image. I wanted to be rough, tough, arrogant, the nigger white folks didn't like' " [*King of the World,* David Remnick, p 224].

Ali had the distinct advantage of being born in 1942, not 1878. He had the advantage of a sports career in the second half of the twentieth century, not the first. And, by instinct or by principle, he seems to have avoided white women entirely.[2]

Of great American heavyweight champions, Jack Johnson (1878–1946) remains sui generis. Though his dazzling and always controversial career reached its zenith in 1910, with Johnson's spectacular defense of his title against the Great White Hope former champion Jim Jeffries, Johnson's poised ring style, his counterpunching speed, precision, and the lethal economy of his punches, seem to us closer in time than the more earnest and forthright styles of Joe Louis, Rocky Marciano, Larry Holmes, Gerry Cooney, et al. That inspired simile "float like a butterfly, sting like a bee," coined to describe the young Cassius Clay/Muhammad Ali in his early dazzling fights, is an apt description of Jack Johnson's cruelly playful dissection of white opponents like Tommy Burns.[3] Ali, a virtuoso of what was called in Johnson's time "mouth-fighting," a continuous barrage of taunts and insults intended to undermine an opponent psychologically, and the inventor of his own, insolently baiting "Ali shuffle," can be seen as a vengeful and victorious avatar of Jack Johnson who perfected the precarious art of playing with and to a hostile audience, like a bullfighter who seduces his clumsy opponent (including the collective "opponent" of the audience) into participating in, in fact heightening, the opponent's own defeat. To step into the ring with a Trickster is to risk not only losing your fight but your dignity.[4]

What was outrageous and "unforgivable" in Johnson's boxing wasn't simply that he so decisively beat his white opponents but that he publicly humiliated them, as a way of demonstrating his smiling, seemingly cordial, contempt for their white constituents. Like Ali, except more astonishing than Ali since Johnson had no predecessors,[5] Johnson transformed formerly capable, formidable opponents into stumbling yokels. Like Ali, Johnson believed in allowing his opponents to wear themselves out in the effort of throwing useless punches. And, like Ali, Johnson understood that boxing is theater. Geoffrey Ward describes the 1909 (mis)match between Johnson and the white middleweight champion Stanley Ketchel in Colma, California:

> For eleven rounds the bout went more or less the way the Burns fight had gone. Johnson towered over his opponent, picking off his punches, smiling and chatting with ringsiders, landing just often and just hard enough to cause Ketchel's mouth and nose to bleed but to do no more serious damage. Several times Johnson simply lifted the smaller man into the air, feet dangling like an oversized doll, and put him down just where he liked. One ringsider called it a "struggle between a demon and a gritty little dwarf."

After a reckless attempt to knock Johnson out, the fight ended brutally for Ketchel with four of his teeth strewn across the ring, or, in variants of the account, embedded in

Johnson's glove, and the hostile crowd silent. After Johnson's equally decisive defeat of the former heavyweight champion Jim Jeffries in 1910, Jeffries was unexpectedly generous in conceding to a reporter, "I could never have whipped Johnson at my best. I couldn't have reached him in a thousand years." More often, white reactions to Johnson's victories were bitter, vicious, hysterical. After Jeffries's defeat, as word of Jack Johnson's victory spread, riots began to break out across the United States. "No event since emancipation forty-five years earlier had meant so much to Negro America as Johnson's victory," Geoffrey Ward notes, "and no event yielded such widespread racial violence until the assassination of Dr. Martin Luther King, Jr., fifty-eight years later." In all, as many as twenty-six people were killed and hundreds more hurt in the rioting, most of them black. In the jubilant wake of this new victory of Jack Johnson's, there would be countless casualties.

Unforgivable Blackness: The Rise and Fall of Jack Johnson is as much a portrait of the boxer's turbulent time as it is of Johnson himself, in the way of such exemplary recent boxing biographies as David Remnick's *King of the World* (1998), which deals with the early, ascending years of Cassius Clay/Muhammad Ali, Roger Kahn's *A Flame of Pure Fire: Jack Dempsey and the Roaring '20s* (1999), and *The Devil and Sonny Liston* (2000) by Nick Tosches, a brilliantly sustained blues piece in prose perfectly matched with its intransigent subject. (Of heavyweight champions,

Liston remains the "taboo" figure: the doomed black man unassimilable by any racial, cultural, or religious collective. Even the nature of Liston's death by heroin overdose— suicide? murder?—remains a mystery.) Ward, author of numerous historical studies including *A First Class Temperament: The Emergence of Franklin Roosevelt* (1989) and a frequent collaborator with the documentary filmmaker Ken Burns on such American subjects as the Civil War, baseball, jazz, Mark Twain, Elizabeth Cady Stanton, and Susan B. Anthony, among others, is both lucky in his biographical subject (Jack Johnson's life even outside the ring reads like a picaresque dime novel) and judicious in his presentation (Johnson's recollections of his life, like those of countless observers, are to be taken with more than a grain of salt). Quite reasonably, Ward focuses upon the phenomenon of Jack Johnson primarily in terms of race, though it might be argued, from a purist boxing standpoint, that Johnson's racial background had no more to do with the elegance and precision of his ring style than any other biographical fact about him.

"Unforgivable blackness" is in reference to a quote from W. E. B. Du Bois in his publication *The Crisis* (1914) with which Ward begins his biography:

> *Boxing has fallen into disfavor . . . The reason is clear: Jack Johnson . . . has out-sparred an Irishman. He did it with little brutality, the utmost fairness and great good nature. He did not "knock" his opponent senseless . . . Neither he nor his race invented prize fighting or*

particularly like it. Why then this thrill of national disgust? Because Johnson is black. Of course some pretend to object to Johnson's character. But we have yet to hear, in the case of White America, that marital troubles have disqualified prize fighters or ball players or even statesmen. It comes down, then, after all to this unforgivable blackness. [p. viii]

(It isn't clear to which fight Du Bois is alluding since Johnson's major fights in 1913–14 took place in Paris and Buenos Aires and it's unlikely that Du Bois saw these fights or even, judging by the broad terms with which he described Johnson's fighting style, that Du Bois ever saw Johnson fight.) Geoffrey Ward notes that, researching the biography, he had no Jack Johnson "papers" to consult apart from such self-mythologizing autobiographies as Johnson's *In the Ring and Out,* and that much of his book is based upon contemporaneous newspaper accounts heavily saturated with "racist contempt." In order to "recapture something of the atmosphere of the world in which [Johnson] always insisted on remaining his own man," Ward resists the "anachronistic term 'African American' " in favor of the one that whites of Johnson's generation used grudgingly and blacks most hoped to see in print: "Negro."

Arthur John Johnson was born in Galveston, Texas, on March 31, 1878, both his parents former slaves. Of the Johnsons' nine children, only four would live to maturity. The third child and first son, Jack was the immediate focus of his family's attention even as, in time, he would seem to have been the focus of attention in virtually every situation, every setting, every gathering in which he was to find himself through most of his life: as naturally charismatic, physically striking and insouciant as Cassius Clay/Muhammad Ali decades later. Like Ali, Jack Johnson was a "cheerful fabulist"—an "inexhaustible tender of his own legend, a teller of tall tales in the frontier tradition of his native state"—as well as a gifted athlete who seems to have seized upon boxing as much as an opportunity to draw attention to himself as a means of making seemingly "easy" money. Unlike Ali, whose I.Q. was once registered as an astonishing 78, and who is said to have been able to read but a small fraction of the voluminous praise and censure heaped on him over the years, Johnson seems to have been an unusually intelligent, articulate, and, to a degree, cultured individual whose emergence out of the Jim Crow South of his era is nothing short of extraordinary.[6] It was Johnson's claim that having been born in the bustling port city of Galveston with its "more relaxed view of racial separation" than that of inland towns and cities of the South accounted for his sense of himself as an individual, and not a member of a racial minority. Long before he became the first Negro heavyweight champion, Jack Johnson knew himself heroic and would have heartily endorsed his biographer's claim that he "embodied American individualism in its purest form; nothing—no law or custom, no person white or black, male or female—could keep him for long from whatever he wanted."

Yet everywhere in the United States, in the North no

less than the South, opportunities for Negro athletes were in fact shrinking. The modest advances that had been made in the late 1800s were being taken back by the passage of Jim Crow laws that allowed white professional baseball players, for instance, to force their black competitors off the field and white jockeys to void licenses held by black jockeys. Even the League of American Wheelmen, Ward wryly notes, banned black bicyclists from their ranks. Boxing remained open to Negroes, but only if they fought other Negroes and didn't aspire to title fights (and the larger purses that came with title fights). In 1895, the prominent newspaperman Charles A. Dana, editor of the *New York Sun,* warned readers: "We are in the midst of a growing menace. The black man is rapidly forging to the front ranks in athletics, especially in the field of fisticuffs. We are in the midst of a black rise against white supremacy."

Yet Jack Johnson began successfully fighting white boxers in San Francisco in the early 1900s and seems to have been from the first a strikingly original, elegant, and elusive counterpuncher given to shrewd theorizing: "By gradually wearing down a fighter, by letting him tire himself out, by hitting him with my left as he came to quarters with me, then by clinching or executing my uppercut, I found that I lasted longer and would not carry any marks out of the ring." Except for carrying a few marks out of the ring, this is a variant of the famous "rope-a-dope" strategy with which Muhammad Ali rewon his heavyweight title from George Foreman in Zaire in October 1974, one of the most astonishing title fights in ring history. It isn't surprising that Jack

Johnson's early hero was the counterpuncher Jim Corbett
whose ring style appeared "scientific" in contrast to the
stiffly upright, crudely aggressive heavyweights of his time,
all forward-lunging offense and no defense, lumbering
strongmen looking for a place to land roundhouse punches.
(As in 1926, in the first of their celebrated title fights, Gene
Tunney would confound the brawling aggressor Jack
Dempsey with a similar "scientific" strategy, landing blows
even as he retreated, gliding "like a great skater on ice" to
win every round of the ten-round fight on points and take
Dempsey's title from him.)[7] In the first film footage showing
Jack Johnson in the ring, a scratchy fragment from the
silent film of Johnson's title fight with Tommy Burns in
1908, we see a tall, unexpectedly graceful heavyweight
with a chiseled upper body, slender waist and legs;
Johnson's head is smooth-shaved and his features might be
described as "sensitive." In the most widely published
photographs of Johnson he as much resembles a dancer as a
heavyweight boxer. (At six feet, weighing a little more than
two hundred pounds, Johnson would be a "small heavyweight" by contemporary standards. Physical size and
strength increased dramatically in the division after 1962,
when super-sized Sonny Liston won the title from the much
smaller Floyd Patterson in arguably the most excruciatingly one-sided title fight in heavyweight boxing history.)
Two years later in his title defense against the much larger
ex-champion Jim Jeffries, Johnson would perform with
equal skill (despite the distracting presence of his old hero
"Gentleman" Jim Corbett striding about at ringside

screaming racist insults at him). Only in the last major fight of his career, against the six-feet-six, two-hundred-thirty-pound White Hope giant Jess Willard in Havana, Cuba, in 1915, did Johnson's counterpunching style fail him: in the famous, or infamous photograph of Jack Johnson lying on his back, Johnson has lifted a gloved hand to shield his eyes from the blinding Caribbean sun, and would afterward claim that he'd thrown the fight.[8]

As heavyweight champion Johnson enjoyed a degree of celebrity unknown to any Negro in previous American history, basking in media attention that kept his handsome, smiling image continuously before the public. Like Muhammad Ali, whose handsome, smiling image would be recognized in parts of the world in which the image of the President of the United States wasn't recognized, Johnson became an icon of his race: "the greatest colored man that ever lived."[9] When not training for an upcoming fight (in gyms and training camps to which the admiring public was invited) he embarked upon theatrical tours across the country. He shadow-boxed, he sparred, he performed in vaudeville and burlesque routines. Here was the very archetype of the "sport"—the dread "flash nigger" made flesh—in ankle-length fur coats, expensive racing cars painted bright colors, tailor-made suits, with rubies, emeralds, diamonds displayed on his elegant person, and the dazzling gold-capped smile for which he was known. (Naturally, Johnson's women were decked in jewels as well. Some of these jewels, Johnson only lent to women for an evening on the town; others were given as gifts to his wives. Etta, the suicidal first

wife, was ensconced in a luxury hotel in London during one
of Johnson's tours of English provincial music halls and
provided with a chauffeur-driven $18,000 royal blue lim-
ousine with $2,500 worth of interior fittings, which seemed
only to increase the unhappy woman's wish to kill herself.)
It was common practice for Johnson to invite (male) journalists to observe him bathing nude and to allow them to
touch his muscled body; his training camps were virtual
open houses for the boxer's self-display, which seemed
never to flag. As a *New York Herald* reporter observed:

> . . . *after the camp is escaped by the visitors Johnson
> discards his smile, forgets his wit and enters upon a
> tirade against the forces that command him to get into
> condition. The champion . . . is a different man when
> he is not showing off to the crowds, the followers, the cu-
> rious, the hero worshippers who create an atmosphere
> which when absent almost seems to leave the negro
> much in the same condition as a lamp would be if the
> oil was taken therefrom. Johnson lives on applause.
> Without it he fades away to nothingness.*

Like Muhammad Ali who compulsively boasted of being
"the greatest"—"the prettiest"—Johnson would seem to
have been the very essence of male narcissism; like Ali,
who would refuse to be drafted into the U.S. Army in the
mid-1960s to fight in Vietnam—"Man, I ain't got no quarrel
with them Vietcong" was Ali's improvised, brilliant rejoin-
der—Jack Johnson incurred the wrath of the majority of his
fellow citizens by declaring in an interview given in London

in 1911, "Fight for America? Well, I should say not. What has America ever done for me or for my race? [In England] I am treated like a human being." Both men would be hounded by righteous white prosecutors, fined and sentenced to federal prison. (Ali's conviction would be overturned by the Supreme Court in 1971. Johnson served his full prison sentence.) Yet the parallel between Ali and Johnson breaks down when one considers their respective attitudes toward their profession, for Ali in his prime was a fanatically disciplined and dedicated boxer whose performances in the ring never failed to transcend the pettiness of his public persona, while Johnson appears not to have finally cared very much about boxing except as a means of celebrity and money-making. Johnson had a notorious penchant for making "deals" (in contrast to "fixing" fights), even when he was heavyweight champion. (The most tempting of deals for the better boxer is simply to carry his opponent through a preplanned number of rounds before knocking him out, for the benefit of gamblers and/or filmmakers, who paid more for more film footage in Johnson's day.) Once he'd achieved a modicum of success, Johnson ceased training seriously for upcoming fights and, sad to say, he managed to avoid leading Negro contenders just as, when Jack Johnson had been the leading contender for the title, the long-reigning Tommy Burns had managed to avoid him.

Geoffrey Ward has divided *Unforgivable Blackness* into two near-equal books: "The Rise" and "The Fall."

Ironically, Johnson's "fall" begins in the immediate after-math of his greatest victory, against Jeffries; it would seem to be inevitable that an individual so driven, for whom self-display is a kind of narcotic, should begin to self-destruct almost immediately after achieving his greatest success. Ward provides a dispiriting catalogue of increasingly pathological behavior on Johnson's part after 1910: heavy drinking, suicidal depression, compulsive gambling and womanizing, violence against his wife Etta, lawsuits, feuds, scandals played out in the media. Only two weeks after the luridly publicized suicide of Etta, Johnson appeared in public in Chicago with a very attractive, very blond eighteen-year-old, an act equivalent to tossing a lighted match into a gasoline drum. (Johnson was thirty-four.) Everywhere Johnson went in the next several years, but es-pecially in the Chicago epicenter, a blaze of notoriety at-tended him; no other boxer except, in our time, the luckless Mike Tyson, has been demonized by the press so relent-lessly. Though Johnson understood that boxing per se has nothing to do with race, only with the performances of often idiosyncratic individuals, he seemed not to wish to under-stand how, even as he used the press as a kind of magnify-ing mirror, the press was using, and exhausting, him.

The Negro pariah, increasingly under attack from both Caucasians and Negroes, somehow managed to escape being assassinated, lynched, or even injured at the hands of white racists, but he could not escape the toxic fallout of public notoriety. In 1913, his enemies literally conspired to trump up criminal charges against him for having allegedly violated the Mann Act (also known as the White Slave Traffic Act of 1909 that barred the "transportation of women in interstate or foreign commerce for the purpose of prostitution or debauchery, or for any other immoral purposes"). Though the law was intended to apply to traffickers in prostitution, not individuals involved in extramarital romances, the Chicago district attorney's office vigorously pursued a criminal case against Johnson based upon the biased and unreliable testimony of a white call girl who'd once been a companion of his:

> *To corroborate and amplify Belle's version of events, federal agents quietly fanned out across the country, interviewing prostitutes, chauffeurs, waiters, bellhops, Pullman porters, ex-managers, former sparring partners, looking for something—anything—that could be used to bolster their case that the champion had broken federal law . . .*

Despite paying out bribes to individuals who might have influenced the outcome of his trial, Johnson was found guilty and sentenced to one year and one day in prison. Though he and his second wife, Lucille—the young blond woman whose presence in Johnson's life had provoked scandal—fled the country and lived abroad for several years, eventually, deep in debt, Johnson returned to the United States to (unsuccessfully) defend his title against the "Pottawatomie Giant" Jess Willard, a lumbering heavyweight with no evident gift for boxing except his size and a reach of eighty-four inches, and to serve his prison sentence in Leavenworth, Kansas, where, true to charismatic form, Johnson made friends not only among his fellow prisoners but among the prison administration, including the white warden who treated his celebrity prisoner with unexpected generosity. Johnson may have been on the downward spiral, an ex-champion in his early forties with no prospects of a title fight from the new champion Dempsey (who had overwhelmed the clumsy Pottawatomie Giant in a fight so bloody it would have been stopped within the first minute of the first round of a contemporary boxing match), yet his leave-taking from Leavenworth was newsworthy:

> Six motion picture cameramen were on hand to capture the moment. Johnson was dressed as only he could dress: straw hat, exquisite tailored gray suit, blinding-white soft-collared shirt, bright polka-dot tie, gleaming patent-leather shoes . . . "There were four bands. Hundreds of people."

At least this is Johnson's account, from his "cheerfully fabulist" autobiography *In the Ring and Out*.

Like many ageing ex-champions, Johnson continued to seek the spotlight that, in his biographer's words, "gave his life meaning." He contracted to appear in a vaudeville company in which, as he boasted, "all the performers except myself were white." He was hired (and very well paid) as a sparring partner for the cocky young Argentine heavyweight Luis Angel Firpo, and soon fired for playing to the crowds gathered in the gym. He toured the boondocks in degrading burlesque revues that called for him, the well-spoken Jack Johnson, to tell jokes in stage-darky dialect. He began drinking heavily. Lucille divorced him but, out of a seemingly endless supply of white women, a third wife, Irene Pineau, almost immediately materialized. At the age of fifty-seven, grudgingly impressed with the boxing skills of the young Joe Louis, Johnson offered to help make a champion of him but was viciously rebuffed by Louis's manager:

> *"He cursed Johnson out," Louis recalled, "told him how he'd held up the progress of the Negro people for years with his attitude, how he was a low-down, no-good nigger and told him he wasn't welcome in my camp any longer."*

To retaliate, Johnson would bet heavily on Max Schmeling to beat Louis in their first fight and, after Schmeling won, boasted so openly of his winnings that he had to be rescued by (white) policemen from a crowd of angry Negroes.

For the remainder of his life Johnson would ply his trade as the ex-first-Negro-heavyweight champion, with diminishing rewards. Well into his sixties he sparred with young boxers, shadow-boxed for whatever public would pay to see him, and impersonated himself in a cellar sideshow off Times Square called Hubert's Museum and Flea Circus. A nightmare end for Jack Johnson, or so it would seem:

> *To see Johnson in person, visitors had to pay a quarter ... Yellowing newspaper clippings from Johnson's ca-*

reer were taped to a booth in which a bored hawker sat making change without looking up . . . Visitors pushed through a little turnstile, made their way down a flight of stairs, and took their seats in the dank, dimly lit cellar. One dreary act followed another—a sword-swallower, a trick dog, a half-man-half-woman . . .

Johnson stepped smoothly onstage, wearing a blue beret, a blue tie, and a worn but sharply cut suit. He held a glass of red wine with a straw in it. He smiled and asked his visitors what they would like to know.

It's true that Joe Louis was a public relations dream, a gifted athlete who acquiesced, as Jack Johnson could never have done, to being made into a "good Negro"—i.e., marketable to a white public; yet in the way of one of those cruelly ironic fairy tales collected by the Brothers Grimm, Louis would find himself in the afterlife of his championship impersonating "Joe Louis" as a greeter at Caesars Palace in Las Vegas: more deeply in debt than Johnson, deeper in despair and sicker.[10] Despite Hubert's Museum and Flea Circus, Johnson seems to have remained supremely himself to the very end: he would die at the age of sixty-eight in an automobile crash outside Raleigh, North Carolina, at the wheel of his high-powered Lincoln Zephyr, reportedly speeding at more than seventy miles an hour. The reason for Johnson's speeding is said to have been indignation that, at a diner, he'd been told he could only eat at the rear.

● ● ●

As the philosopher is susceptible to sometimes disappearing into such abstraction that his subject can seem nugatory—quite literally "nothing"—so the historian at his most generous can assemble so many facts, details, quotations that the reader becomes lost in a plethora of "somethings." Since *Unforgivable Blackness* is likely to be the definitive biography of Jack Johnson, the absence of a chronology of Johnson's fact-filled life is unfortunate. Often, in medias res, it's difficult to figure out the year without consulting the index, to determine when a newspaper article appeared. Most readers of a boxing biography can be assumed to have more than a passing interest in boxing, yet Ward doesn't include a record of his subject's boxing career, a frustrating and inexplicable omission. (In sharply abbreviated form, Johnson's record is 113 fights: 79 wins, 12 draws, 8 losses, 14 no decisions. Compare Jack Dempsey with 80 fights: 61 wins, 7 draws, 7 losses, 5 no decisions, and 1 no contest; Joe Louis with 70 fights: 67 wins, 3 losses; Muhammad Ali with 61 fights: 56 wins, 5 losses.) Also, the biography ends somewhat too abruptly with Johnson's death and funeral: we feel the need for an epilogue to provide an overview of Johnson's legacy, historic and mythic. No sport is more mindful of its iconic past than boxing and at a time when even the outlaw figure of Sonny Liston is being revalued, Johnson merits this consideration.

In any case, *Unforgivable Blackness* is a significant achievement. Geoffrey Ward provides an utterly convincing and frequently hearttrending portrait of Jack Johnson, "the man with the golden smile," for whom the ideal representa-

tion would be the Janus-face of simultaneous comedy and
tragedy.

NOTES

1. After Johnson lost the heavyweight title to Jess Willard
in 1915, the title would be held by white boxers until 1937, when
twenty-three-year-old Joe Louis became champion. The shrewd
(white) managers of Joe Louis, who made his pro boxing debut in
1934 when the thorny memory of Jack Johnson still rankled in
the public's memory, drew up a list of specific rules for Louis: he
was never to have his picture taken with a white woman; he was
never to go into a nightclub alone; he would be involved in no
"soft" fights, and no "fixed" fights; he was never to gloat over a
fallen opponent; he was to "live clean and fight clean." Arguably
a greater heavyweight than Jack Johnson, certainly one with a
more impressive record of victories over worthy opponents, Joe
"The Brown Bomber" Louis became an American sports success
of immense natural talent shaped and controlled by marketing
strategies. Though Louis ended his career humiliated and broken, owing back taxes on even the "income" of two purses he'd
naively donated to the war effort in the early 1940s, addicted to
cocaine, and plagued by the paranoid, but not inaccurate, suspi-
cion that the FBI had him under surveillance, yet in public memory he continues to occupy a mythic identity as the "good"
American Negro heavyweight champion who beat the "Nazi"
Max Schmeling in 1938. Though ironic in terms of Louis's personal life, that of the exploited Negro athlete, this entry from the

Encyclopedia of Boxing is accurate: "[Louis's] exemplary behavior both in and out of the ring sharply raised the prestige of black boxers."

2. Since Muhammad Ali has become a totemic figure in the pantheon of American folk heroes, no one wishes to recall how in the 1960s and 1970s, a convert to the Nation of Islam ("Black Muslims" in the white press) and an outspoken critic of American culture, Ali was regularly booed at fights and chided, if not vilified, in print. TV commentators and numerous publications including the *New York Times* refused to call him anything other than "Casius Clay." On his part, Ali was a vehement black racist who believed in the subjection of Muslim women to Muslim men and an absolute division of the races: "A black man should be killed if he's messing with a white woman . . . [If a Muslim woman consorts with white men] then *she* dies. Kill her, too." (*Playboy* interview, November 1975.)

3. In an era in which title fights were scheduled for twenty rounds, the fight with Burns was stopped abruptly in the fourteenth round when Sydney police officers, agitated that the Negro challenger was winning, entered the ring. Burns would afterward protest that, if the police hadn't interfered, "I might even have won because the big nigger was tiring fast." [p. 127] Contemporary title fights are twelve rounds. (Most fights are eight or ten rounds and all are closely monitored by ringside physicians, unheard-of in Jack Johnson's time.)

4. See Gerald Early, "The Black Intellectual and the Sport of Prizefighting": "Against black opponents the white yokels were not even really fighters; they were more like preservers of the white public's need to see Tricksters pay a price for their dis-

order." (*Speech and Power*, Vol. 1, 1992, edited by Gerald Early.) Ali is the supreme heavyweight Trickster even as, paradoxically, no one has been more purely devoted to boxing:

> [Ali] forced us to reimagine the ways an athlete moves through time and space; even in his waning years, he waged a battle against stylistic norms. As a youth he held his hands too low, and yanked his head straight back from blows (an amateurish move, the traditionalists grumbled) yet he so accelerated the pace of heavyweight fighting that scarcely anyone could keep up with him. With extraordinary self-consciousness, Ali relished the difficulty his dancing around and back created not only for his opponent, but also for ringside cameramen trying to keep him in the frame. As he aged, he sought the opposite extreme in posture and pacing: immobile along the ropes, head down and hands held low, he slowed the pace of major fights to an excruciating point, exhausting his foes . . . Ali was always the expert parodist, whether through his cartoonlike nicknames for his opponents' styles ("The Rabbit," "The Octopus," "The Washerwoman"), or through his exaggerated mirrorings of his foe . . . These moves gave Ali the illusion of omnipotence, even when he had to struggle.
>
> —RONALD LEVAO, "Reading the Fights,"
> *Raritan*, spring 1986

5. Johnson had no Negro Trickster predecessors but of course he had Negro predecessors in the literal sense, foremost among them the West Indian-born heavyweight Peter Jackson (1861–1901). Jackson was the best Negro boxer of his era and

very likely would have beaten John L. Sullivan if Sullivan, an avowed white racist, had granted him a title fight. (Sullivan was the reigning "Prize Ring" champion from 1882 to 1892, when boxers still fought bare-knuckled.) Even after Jackson fought James Corbett to a draw in a four-hour, sixty-one-round fight, Sullivan refused to fight him. Previously, Sullivan had refused to fight another leading Negro contender named George Godfrey. White champions commonly "drew the color line" against Negros out of a fear that, like Tommy Burns, they would be humiliated in the ring. Until the rise of Joe Louis in the 1930s, a white champion like Jack Dempsey could avoid Negro boxers through an entire career. For this reason, the history of boxing before Louis is not an authentic history. As Peter Jackson was the "shadow" champion during the reign of John L. Sullivan so the Negro Harry Wills was the "shadow" champion during the reign of Jack Dempsey. In his widely publicized pursuit of Tommy Burns, in which he enlisted the white press on his behalf, Jack Johnson broke the mold of Negro boxers like Jackson who behaved with public deference to whites. Johnson would have perceived that being a "good" Negro would get him no further than Jackson and Godfrey: being a "white man's Negro" wasn't for him. Negro athletes like Peter Jackson were extolled by such Negro leaders as Booker T. Washington and Frederick Douglass; the Negro historian James Weldon Johnson compared Peter Jackson favorably to Jack Johnson, noting that Jackson's deportment in public and chivalry in the ring had brought him the compliment from white sportswriters that he was a "white colored man." [Quoted in *King of the World* by David Remnick, p. 277]

6. White journalists were continually being surprised by Jack Johnson the "complex, mercurial man behind the grin." [p. 187] A Baltimore *American* reporter notes, in 1910:

... once in his private quarters the negro became a changed man. He ordered one of his assistants to load the phonograph, and for an hour the hotel was filled with the strains of operatic music, vocal selections rendered by Caruso and others ... Not once did a "ragtime" piece appear ... In another corner there stood an immense bass viol. Somebody asked casually who played it, and Johnson said, "I do. Like to hear me?" [p. 187]

Another observer notes that Johnson is "no stranger in the world of books and writers":

He browsed through books on all subjects—fiction, science, art, history; he has read them in three languages— English, French, and Spanish. He is conversant with works of Shakespeare ... When discussing books and the names of Alexander Dumas and Victor Hugo are mentioned, Johnson becomes more alert than ever, for these are two of his favorite writers ... While his schooling was interrupted before he reached high school, he has nevertheless attained an education of thoroughgoing character ... He is a musician of no mean ability, his favorite instrument being the bass viol, which he plays in a talented manner.

—quoted in JERVIS ANDERSON, "Black Heavies," in *Speech and Power* Vol. 1

7. The remark is Dempsey's. For a detailed description of this famous fight see *A Flame of Pure Desire: Jack Dempsey and the Roaring '20's* by Roger Kahn, p. 399.

8. Though Johnson seems to have acknowledged immediately after the fight that he'd legitimately lost ("I met a young big boy and he wore me down. I didn't dream there was a man alive who could go fifteen rounds with me once I started after him" [p. 380]), he would afterward claim that he'd thrown the fight in a deal that would have allowed him to return to the United States without having to serve a prison sentence (for his 1913 conviction of having violated the Mann Act). The deal evidently fell through, since Johnson had to serve his sentence, and the mystery of the fight remains open to speculation. If Johnson was intending to lose, he put up a convincing fight for more than twenty rounds in the blistering Havana, Cuba, sunshine, before visibly tiring and losing his strength. The famous photograph of Johnson lying on his back on the canvas at the end of the twenty-sixth round [as if languidly lifting his gloved hand to shield his eyes from blinding sunshine] does have a fraudulent look to it, however. (Though Sonny Liston eerily replicated this scene in 1965, in the first round of his infamous rematch with heavyweight champion Muhammad Ali, knocked out by an infamous "shadow punch" that hardly looks powerful enough to have cost him the fight, Liston probably had not intended a postmodernist reference to his great predecessor.)

9. Seven decades later, in a Catskill training camp overseen by the legendary trainer Cus D'Amato, the sixteen-year-old Mike Tyson took note:

Tyson marveled at Jack Johnson, the most famous of black heavyweight champions, who caught punches with his open glove, talked to people in the stands during the fight, and laughed in the faces of his hapless opponents . . . He found out that among the fighters of the 1920s gold teeth were a status symbol, and had two of his upper front teeth capped in gold.

—*Mike Tyson: Money, Myth and Betrayal*
by MONTIETH ILLINGWORTH (1991), pp. 5–56

10. The pathos of Joe Louis's later life is belied by the tone of his ghost-written memoir, *My Life* (1978), in which the ravages of Louis's ill health, mental instability, and financial distress are adroitly glossed over. Though only in his early sixties, Louis has become an elderly, addled mascot in the employ of a gambling casino:

Yeah, I'm comfortable in Vegas. Don't have to get dressed up . . . just wear a sport shirt, of course, most times it's silk, cowboy hat or baseball cap, slacks, sometimes my cowboy boots . . . I see all my old friends when they come to entertain. Frank Sinatra and me go back a long time.

—*Joe Louis: My Life* (1978), p. 261

THE AVENGER

JOE LOUIS
VS.
MAX SCHMELING

Boxing is the most pitiless of sports, as it can be the most dazzling, theatrical and emblematic. Where race and nationalism are involved, as in the famous Joe Louis-Max Schmeling heavyweight fights of 1936 and 1938, two of the most widely publicized boxing matches in history, the emblematic aspect of the sport can assume epic proportions. When the second fight, of June 1938, pitting the twenty-four-year-old American Negro titleholder, Louis, against the thirty-two-year-old Schmeling, the Nazis' star athlete, was fought at Yankee Stadium, the contest was as much between the United States and Nazi Germany as between two superbly skilled athletes. There were almost seventy thousand spectators and an estimated one hundred million radio listeners throughout the world: "the largest audience in history for *anything*."

David Margolick, the author of such diverse works of nonfiction as *Strange Fruit: The Biography of a Song*, *At the Bar: The Passions and Peccadilloes of American Lawyers*, and *Undue Influence: The Epic Battle Over the Johnson & Johnson Fortune*, is clearly disadvantaged in retelling so familiar a sports tale. The Louis-Schmeling

• *261* •

fights, with their extraordinary political/cultural significance, have been analyzed more than any other boxing
matches in history; the paired fights have become staples of
ESPN Classic; there have been TV documentaries on Louis
and Schmeling as iconic representatives of their nations in
the years preceding World War II, inevitably covering the
same historical ground. The most poignant and engaging of
recent books to examine the role of Joe Louis in the politi-
cized epic drama is Donald McRae's *Heroes Without a
Country: America's Betrayal of Joe Louis and Jesse Owens*
(2003).

What Margolick has accomplished in *Beyond Glory* is
to provide an exhaustively researched background to the
Louis-Schmeling rivalry that includes sympathetic portraits
of both Joe Louis and Max Schmeling; an examination of
racism at home and anti-Semitism in Germany; a look at the
predominant role of Jews in professional boxing in the
United States; and, interlarded through the text, opinions by
just about anyone, from boxing experts and sportswriters to
celebrities and ordinary, anonymous citizens, who might
have had something to say about Louis or Schmeling that
found its way into print, valuable or otherwise. Less cultural
criticism than Margolick's artfully focused *Strange Fruit*,
Beyond Glory is historical reportage, a heavyweight of a book
that is likely to be the definitive chronicle of its subject.

"Too good to be true, and absolutely true . . . the most
beautiful fighting machine that I have ever seen": so Ernest
Hemingway famously wrote of Joe Louis after the twenty-
one-year-old's savage victory over the ex-heavyweight

champion Max Baer in 1935. Louis's distinctive ring style, like the politely inexpressive public persona cultivated for him by his canny managers, gave the impression of robotlike precision, the more lethal for being seemingly without emotion. "Joe Louis ain't no natural killer," Louis's trainer remarked. "He's a manufactured killer." In both Louis-Schmeling fights, with their singularly different outcomes—Louis was ignominiously knocked out by Schmeling in the twelfth round of the first fight; in the rematch, Louis knocked Schmeling out in a spectacular feat of boxing, in the first round—the young black heavyweight was as impressive for the devastating accuracy of his fists as for his economical footwork and the power of his combination punches. A "small" heavyweight by contemporary, post–Sonny Liston standards at 6 feet 1¾ inches, with a reach of 76 inches and, in 1936, weighing 198 pounds, Louis had disproportionately large hands and powerfully muscled wrists, forearms and legs; in his celebrated early fights, available on film, he more resembles a twenty-first-century middleweight than a heavyweight. You can see how, in the 1936 match with Schmeling, Louis's inexperience cost him the fight: the German boxer had scrutinized films of Louis's fights and discovered a habitual weakness in his defense, an unconscious lowering of his left glove after throwing a punch. (In more colloquial terms, the Cinderella Man, James J. Braddock, heavyweight champion from 1935 to 1937, thought Louis was "a sucker for a right hand; every time he jabbed he leaned way over and stuck his kisser out there, just begging to be socked.") By the time of the media-hyped rematch on June 22, 1938—"Joe Louis versus Adolf Hitler Day"—Louis had been trained not to make that mistake, with devastating results for his older opponent. The victory of the American "Brown Bomber" over the German "altar to manliness" was so decisive that even the suspicious German press, after examining fight films, could not contest it.

At the time of his initial retirement in 1949, Joe Louis had a brilliant ring record of sixty wins—fifty-one by knockout—and one loss, through a career of fifteen years that included twenty-five title defenses. Along with his controversial predecessor Jack Johnson, the first black heavyweight champion (1908–15), and his yet more famous successor Muhammad Ali (1964–67; 1974–78; 1978–79), Louis ranks with the greatest heavyweight boxers in history, of a stature surpassing that of, for instance, Rocky Marciano, who defeated him in 1951 after Louis's ill-advised comeback. Like many former champions, Louis was forced to resume his career for financial reasons, with humiliating results. His accounts had been so mismanaged that though he'd reputedly earned $4.6 million by the late 1940s, Louis had virtually nothing to show for it. (In a gesture of patriotic but naive generosity, he had donated the purses of two of his fights to the United States war effort in the early 1940s, for which the IRS relentlessly hounded him for taxes and arrears amounting to nearly a half-million dollars, a colossal debt at midcentury.) As in the grimmest of fairy tales, the most honored athlete of his time, the man responsible for "the greatest show of Negro unity America

had ever seen," would end his career as a professional
wrestler, then a "greeter" at Caesars Palace in Las Vegas,
where, drug-dependent and paranoid, he would die of car-
diac arrest and general physical collapse in 1981, at the
age of sixty-six.

By contrast, and ironically, the ever-resourceful,
chameleonlike and urbane Max Schmeling not only survived the brutal vicissitudes of the boxing ring and the
trauma of his 1938 defeat but was able to maintain his
reputation as a homeland hero—"German Champion in
All Classes"—through a lengthy, perennially public career
of self-promotion and self-mythologizing. As Margolick
writes, "The man who was malleable enough to fit into
Weimar Germany and the Third Reich with equal ease now
became an exemplar of West Germany, of its economic mir-
acle and its fledgling democracy." Schmeling would live to
be ninety-nine; he would die a millionaire.

Where Joe Louis gives the impression of being, for all
his dominance in the ring, essentially passive and susceptible to manipulation by others (see *Joe Louis: My Life*, by
Joe Louis with Edna and Art Rust Jr., 1978), Max Schmeling appears to have been the consummate manipulator of
others. In appearance, in boxing trunks, Schmeling more
resembled the Manassa Mauler, Jack Dempsey, than an
emblem of fair Aryan manhood, but his ring style was the
antithesis of Dempsey's unstoppered aggression: "cooler,
slower, more methodical—'Teutonic.'" As a young man
Schmeling had taken pride in associating with German in-

tellectuals like the filmmaker Josef von Sternberg, the artist
George Grosz and Thomas Mann's novelist brother, Hein-
rich Mann: "Artists, grant me your favor—boxing is also an
art!" he wrote to one of these. Shrewd enough never to have
joined the Nazi Party, in part because he was depending
upon American (i.e., Jewish-managed) boxing for a lucrative career, Schmeling yet benefited from the patronage of
the highest-ranking Nazis and the admiration of Hitler; in
the United States he emphasized the separation of politics
and sports, as in Germany he readily gave the Nazi salute
and acquiesced in the "Nazification" of athletics. His can-
niest decision was to have signed a contract as a relatively
young boxer to fight in America under the auspices of Joe
Jacobs, the Jewish manager with whom he would remain
through the anti-Semitic ravages of the Third Reich. As
Margolick notes: "He had the best of both worlds: he was
making enormous amounts of money . . . and had the ap-
probation of his people and his government. There is no
evidence, in anything he said or did at the time, to suggest that he ever agonized over anything." Schmeling's
greatest coup, more lucrative than any boxing purse, was
being offered a Coca-Cola dealership in northern Germany that would make him wealthy in the very years when
Joe Louis, whom the Atlanta-based company had never
wished to approach for advertising purposes, was crushed
by debt.

When American boxing was at its zenith in the first
half of the twentieth-century, as Margolick says, "Jews were
all over boxing, not just as fighters and fans but . . . promot-

ers, trainers, managers, referees, propagandists, equipment manufacturers, suppliers, chroniclers." (Jewish boxers? The most famous were the lightweight champions Benny Leonard and Barney Ross. Marketable Jewish heavyweights were in such short supply that the non-Jewish Max Baer, a charismatic champion of 1934–35, performed in trunks adorned with the Star of David.) Through their careers Louis and Schmeling were associated with Jewish boxing entrepreneurs, both named Jacobs: Mike, Joe. Not only were the two Jacobses unrelated but the men were temperamental opposites: Mike Jacobs the dour, humorless fight promoter whom few liked, Joe Jacobs the "quintessential Broadway guy" liked even by men who didn't trust him. Where Joe Jacobs was "fanatically devoted to his fighters, whom he championed unceasingly and ingeniously," Mike Jacobs took so little interest in his boxers that he sometimes didn't trouble to watch even their championship matches: "For him, the real sport lay in staging a show, outwitting the other guy, putting fannies in seats. . . . Fight nights he could often be seen patrolling the stadium, or even hawking tickets." Yet "Uncle Mike" was the individual responsible for Joe Louis's phenomenal career, financing the young boxer at the start and grooming him for the championship by assuring that Louis would be marketed to the white public in a way to neutralize the image of the flamboyant Jack Johnson. Margolick writes:

> *Louis would be the antithesis of everything Jack Johnson had been. He would always be softspoken, under-*

stated and polite, no matter what he accomplished. He would not preen or gloat or strut in the ring. . . . He would always conduct himself with dignity. . . . When it came to women, he would stick to his own kind. . . . He would never fraternize with white women, let alone be photographed with them. He would not drive fast cars, especially red ones. . . . The press would be saturated with stories of Louis's boyish goodness, his love for his mother, his mother's love for him, his devotion to Scripture.

Without this discreetly constructed persona, which accounts for Louis's "frozen" demeanor in public, it's probable that Joe Louis would be recalled as one of the legendary "shadow champions" like Peter Jackson and Harry Wills, black boxers whom the champions John L. Sullivan and Jack Dempsey managed to avoid.

Joe Jacobs, Schmeling's ever-zealous manager, was also concerned with honoring marketable images for his fighters. He was scrappy, bright, inventive and courageous or reckless enough to take one of his fighters to Georgia, where Jacobs was threatened by the Ku Klux Klan. The anti-Semitic newspaper columnist Westbrook Pegler called him "a New York sidewalk boy of the most conspicuous Jewishness," but fight folks called him "Yussel the Muscle." In a time in which activist Jews were organizing boycotts of German goods and of individuals like Max Schmeling, Joe Jacobs came to the seeming defense of Nazi

Germany: "Most of the trouble with the Jews over there is caused by the Jews in this country." In a comic-nightmare episode like a scene from a Woody Allen movie, after a victory of Schmeling's in Hamburg in 1935 the wily Jew from New York City found himself hauled into the ring by Schmeling as the German national anthem was being sung by twenty-five thousand ecstatic Germans lifting their arms in the Nazi salute:

"Jacobs was momentarily at a loss. But everyone else was saluting, he thought, and he was in plain sight; what else was he to do? So up went his right arm, too, though with a cigar nestled between his fingers. . . . Schmeling's arm was stiff and resolute, while Jacobs's was more limp, as if halfheartedly hailing a cab."

Joe Jacobs would die of a heart attack at forty-two in 1940, not long after his star boxer had left boxing to become a paratrooper in the Wehrmacht.

The actual time a boxer spends fighting is minuscule set beside the interminable preparation, training, "intrigue and . . . politicking" of the kind Margolick reports in detail, so in *Beyond Glory* the Louis-Schmeling fights take up a very small part of the text. Most of the chapters are impersonal historical accounts, culled from numerous sources, in which the author's voice is subordinate to his material. Amid much summarizing, press clippings of the era, many of them painfully racist, provide candor and color; occasionally there are outbursts of a kind of comic surrealism, as in this rapid collage following the dramatic outcome of the 1938 fight:

In the stands there was bedlam. Tallulah Bankhead sprang to her feet and turned to the Schmeling fans behind her. "I told you so, you sons of bitches!" she screamed. Whites were hugging blacks. "The happiest people I saw at this fight were not the Negroes but the Jews," a black writer observed. "In the row in front of me there was a great line of Jews—and they had the best time of all their Jewish lives." . . . "Beat the hell out of the damn German bastard!" W. E. B. Du Bois, a lifelong Germanophile who rarely swore, shouted gleefully in Atlanta. In Hollywood, Bette Davis jumped up and down; she had won $66 in the Warner Brothers fight pool . . . "Everybody danced and sang." Woody Guthrie wrote from Santa Fe. "I watched the people laugh, walk, sing, do all sorts of dances. I heard 'Hooray for Joe Louis!' 'To hell with Max Schmeling' in Indian, Mexican, Spanish, all kinds of white tongues."

(Here is history as antic folk art, like a mural by Thomas Hart Benton.)

Beyond an ambitious distillation of facts and a blizzard of opinions, what seems missing in *Beyond Glory* is authorial perspective: what does David Margolick make of the Louis-Schmeling phenomenon? Are such crude but potent myths of the "moral" superiority of physical superiority still dominant in our culture? Did not a single commentator among so many make the obvious point that Joe Louis beat Max Schmeling in the ring because, that night, he was the better boxer, not because he was the better man, or represented the better country? Did not one commentator take note that boxing, like warfare, has nothing to do with virtue? Even in the epilogue the author's voice is curiously muted, where one might expect some of the subtly nuanced, informed and engaging commentary that gives such life to *At the Bar* (1995), a collection of Margolick's legal columns from the *New York Times*.

Yet *Beyond Glory* is a valuable addition to a growing library of books on sports and culture, one to set beside Gerald Early's *Culture of Bruising* (1994) and Geoffrey C. Ward's *Unforgivable Blackness: The Rise and Fall of Jack Johnson* (2004) as a chronicle of an era not so bygone as we might wish.

ACKNOWLEDGMENTS

Anderson, Dave. *In The Corner: Great Boxing Trainers Talk About Their Art* (William Morrow, New York, 1991).

Anderson, Dave. Articles in *The New York Times*.

Berger, Phil. Articles in *The New York Times*.

Collins, Nigel. "Mike Tyson: The Legacy of Cus D'Amato," *The Ring,* February 1986.

Early, Gerald. *Tuxedo Junction: Essays on American Culture* (The Ecco Press, New Jersey, 1989).

Fried, Ronald K. *Corner Men: Great Boxing Trainers* (Four Walls, Eight Windows, New York, 1991).

Gorn, Elliot J. "The Manassa Mauler and the Fighting Marine: An Interpretation of the Dempsey-Tunney Fights," *Journal of American Studies,* Vol. 19 (1985).

Hauser, Thomas. *Muhammad Ali: His Life and Times* (Simon & Schuster, New York, 1991).

Hauser, Thomas. *The Black Lights: Inside the World of Pro-*

fessional Boxing (Simon & Schuster, New York, 1986, 1991).

Heller, Peter. *In This Corner: Forty World Champions Tell Their Stories* (Simon & Schuster, New York, 1973).

Illingworth, Montieth. *Mike Tyson: Money, Myth and Betrayal* (Birch Lane Press, New York, 1991).

McCallum, John D. *The World Heavyweight Boxing Championship: A History* (Chilton Book Co., Radnor, Pennsylvania, 1974).

McIlvanney, Hugh. *McIlvanney on Boxing: An Anthology* (Beaufort Books, New York, 1983).

Mead, Chris. *Champion: Joe Louis; Black Hero in White America* (Charles Scribner's Sons, New York, 1985).

Odd, Gilbert. *Encyclopedia of Boxing* (Crescent Books, New York, 1983).

The Ring magazine (New York, New York).

Schulian, John. *Writers' Fighters and Other Sweet Scientists* (Andrews & McMeel, Fairway, Kansas, 1983).

Background material for the section on "opponents" was drawn from articles by Michael Shapiro and Budd Schulberg appearing in *The New York Times* and *Newsday* respectively.

Sociologists David P. Phillips and John E. Hensley in "When Violence Is Rewarded or Punished: The Impact of Mass Media Stories on Homicide," *Journal of Communication,* Summer 1984, argue that highly publicized boxing matches have a direct and measurable effect upon the homicide rate, albeit with curious qualifications of race.

I am deeply indebted to my friend Ronald Levao of Rutgers University, who made available to me much of his collection of films and tapes of boxing matches from Johnson-Ketchel, 1909, to the present time, and whose advice and encouragement in the preparation of the manuscript has been invaluable.

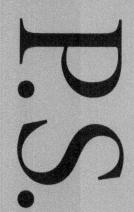

About the author

About the book

Read on

Insights,
Interviews
& More . . .

Profile of Joyce Carol Oates

by Eithne Farry

ON THE WALL above Joyce Carol Oates's desk is a 1957 quote from the film director Alfred Hitchcock. It says: "It's only a movie, let's not go too deeply into these things." These simple words of advice were given to Kim Novak when she was feeling agitated and despondent on the set of *Vertigo*. "I thought it was good advice," says Joyce Carol Oates. "Writers can get too intense and too emotionally involved with their work. Sometimes I tend to get a little anxious and nervous about my writing, and I can make myself unhappy, so I look up at that quote and think, it's only a book, don't worry, it's not your life."

Marion Ettlinger

But writing is an intrinsic part of Joyce Carol Oates's life, the biographical details overshadowed by her literary output. To date, Oates has thirty-nine novels, nineteen collections of short stories, and numerous plays and nonfiction works (including monographs on boxing and the American artist George Bellows) to her name—as well as the novels of her pseudonyms Rosamond Smith and Lauren Kelly. By the time this interview appears that number, in all likelihood, will have increased. "I like writing, and I'm always working on something; if it's not a novel, then it'll be a short story, or an essay, or a book review."

From an early age Oates was fascinated by

words; she began writing when she was very young. "Even before I could write I was emulating adult handwriting. So I began writing, in a sense, before I was able to write." Her first stories were about cats and horses. "I love animals. I'm very close to animals." Born on Bloomsday—June 16, 1938—she grew up on a small farm in Lockport, New York, and studied at the same one-room school her mother attended. Her grandparents had a hard life: Joyce's father and his mother moved frequently "from one low-priced rental to another"; Joyce's mother was handed over to the care of an aunt when her father died suddenly and left the family impoverished. "Is 'die' too circumspect a term?" asks Oates. "In fact, my maternal grandfather was killed in a tavern brawl."

Oates is the eldest of three and her childhood territory was mapped out in books. She was a voracious reader; by the time she was in her teens she was devouring Henry David Thoreau, Hemingway, Emily Brontë, Faulkner—and she can track the influence of these major writers in her own work. She explains: "I think we are most influenced when we are adolescents. Whoever you read when you're fifteen, sixteen, seventeen, eighteen are probably the strongest influences of your whole life." She adds, "I think it's true for all artists: as an adolescent you don't have much background, you don't know much. I can imagine a young artist who's, say, thirteen years old and seeing Cézanne for the first time being very, very overwhelmed. But it's not going to have the same impact when you're forty."

Oates majored in English at Syracuse University (to which she won a scholarship) and won the *Mademoiselle* "college short story" competition in 1959, when she was just nineteen (Sylvia Plath received this coveted award in 1951). She gained her master's degree from the University of Wisconsin in just a ▶

> 'Even before I could write I was emulating adult handwriting. So I began writing, in a sense, before I was able to write.'

> [Oates] won the *Mademoiselle* 'college short story' competition in 1959, when she was just nineteen (Sylvia Plath received this coveted award in 1951).

year, and had already embarked on her prolific writing career at this point, at times publishing two or three books in the space of twelve months. In 1962 she and her husband Raymond Smith moved to Detroit and stayed there until 1968, witnessing at first hand the civil unrest that overtook many American cities. She was "shaken" by the experience, and "brooded upon it." She is now a professor at Princeton, but the violence and unease of the Detroit years still make their unnerving way into her fiction more than forty years later.

The sheer amount of Oates's output can be bewildering. Her biographer Greg Johnson recalls his first visit to the Oates archive at Syracuse University, when he was beginning research for *The Invisible Woman,* his book on Oates. "My overwhelming impression was of the sheer amount of labor represented by these manuscripts . . . the novel manuscripts in particular were astonishing in their complexity." Oates explains, "I like writing. I'm not a person who thinks in terms of her career. I think in terms of the work I'm doing." She adds, "I don't think I'm incredibly disciplined. I write in the mornings, I sometimes write through the afternoon, even the evening, but not every day. It's not a schedule that's rigid."

Her earlier fiction was written in "one headlong plunge," a rush of words across the page. Then she would "systematically rewrite the entire manuscript, first word to last . . . and this was the triumph of Art . . . control imposed upon passion." Oates still writes every manuscript in longhand first, and then continues her work on a typewriter, editing each book as many as five times before she is happy with it. "I don't have a computer. And I won't let things go until I'm happy." She doesn't have hobbies, but likes to run, hike and cycle in the summer, before heading back to

> 66 Oates . . . writes every manuscript in longhand first, and then continues her work on a typewriter, editing each book as many as five times before she is happy with it. 99

the study to get back to her writing. "I'm just trying to do the best work I can. Most writers are trying to do the best they can. You hope someone responds to the work, but then you move on to a new project." It's a pragmatic attitude to a prolific career. "People can get depressed and suicidal and upset with their work, but I look at that Hitchcock quote on my wall and remind myself it's only a book, don't worry, it's not your life. It's a good cautionary tale." ∽

A Conversation with Joyce Carol Oates

What initially interested you in boxing, so unlikely a sport for a woman to have immersed herself in?

When I was a young girl, my father, Frederic Oates, took me to Golden Gloves boxing tournaments in Buffalo, New York. In the large, smoke-filled arena, for this was a time when the concept "smoke-free" no more existed than the wistful concept "women's rights," I was one of relatively few girls and women. At the age of ten or eleven, in my father's company, I was made to feel privileged; yet, as my father was sitting with his men friends and their sons, and the young boxers were male, I was made to feel distinctly "other."

Do you think that there is an innate gender difference between men and women in terms of sports?

It has usually been a principle that the rougher and more dangerous the sport, the more "masculine" the sport is. Whether this is an innate principle or one that is culturally determined isn't clear. Boxing has traditionally been associated with extremely poor and socially disenfranchised young men seeking to remedy, in the ring, the injustices of their lives. Only in recent decades has boxing become slightly less dangerous: overseen by ring physicians, for instance, and monitored by physical examinations and boxing licenses. Yet there is still an air of the desperate about boxing, which Mike Tyson once said was, to his way of thinking, not a "sport" but something more akin to ancient Roman gladiatorial combat. There is no reason why women can't be boxers, and very good boxers; but the social and cultural impetus isn't there, to any degree. The average woman (if there is an "average" woman!) doesn't derive any pleasure from seeing two individuals involved in an intense, concentrated effort to knock one another out; women tend to identify, as I often do, with the losing boxer, feeling an involuntary stab of empathy with this boxer's pain and loss of control. The average man will feel a sensation of pleasure at the dominance of the winning boxer, for there can be something beautiful in the execution of such skills; a triumph over the physical limitations of the self, perhaps. Men tend to "identify" with winners, and to feel embarrassment, chagrin, even contempt for losers.

Do you think that there is something unique to boxing?

Boxing seems to us a paradigm of life: the unpredictable, the possibly tragic. Boxing is a mimicry of a fight to the death, a theatrical sort of mortal combat. While such sports as tennis, golf, and chess are game versions of combat, boxing is not a game but the real thing. It inhabits a particular dimension in sports history for this reason.

What excites you about boxing, as a writer?

The personalities of boxers, one might say their "destinies," are of exceptional interest: such individuals as Jack Johnson, Jack Dempsey, Joe Louis, Rocky Marciano, Jake LaMotta, Sugar Ray Robinson, Muhammad Ali, Mike Tyson are, quite simply, larger than life. Their histories are emblematic of much more than their individual lives, it seems; their relationship with the politics and culture of their eras, their role in the ongoing "racial drama" of America, are fascinating.

You've been quoted as saying that boxing is more about failure than success. ▶

❝ Women tend to identify, as I often do, with the losing boxer, feeling an involuntary stab of empathy with this boxer's pain and loss of control. The average man will feel a sensation of pleasure at the dominance of the winning boxer. ❞

A Conversation with Joyce Carol Oates
(continued)

Most boxers fail, most of the time. Even the great champions—Dempsey, Louis, Ali, Jack Johnson—and the near-great, like Tyson—can suffer terrible humiliations in the ring. (Only Rocky Marciano, who trained obsessively and exhaustively, quit boxing while undefeated; not because he feared defeat, but because the training was so arduous, like training in no other sport.)

What boxers and fights have you admired?

Obviously, I've written at length about Muhammad Ali, the greatest heavyweight boxer in history, whose major fights have become classics in the sport. One of the things I liked about Sugar Ray Leonard was that, like all great boxers, he was most dangerous after he'd been knocked down. Once the average boxer is knocked down, something goes out of him. But when Leonard was knocked down and then would get up he was much more dangerous than before. I liked Leonard near the end of his career a lot more than I liked him earlier. Like many people, I wanted Marvin Hagler to win their fight and couldn't believe it when Hagler lost. Looking back, we might say that Hagler's finest moment—when he fought Tommy Hearns—turned him into a lesser boxer because of the beating he took from the man he beat. If Hagler had fought a different fight he might have beat Hearns anyway, but he would not have been hurt as much. They both took terrible beatings. That was a fantastic fight.

Have you written very much about boxing, in your novels and short stories?

You Must Remember This is my novel "about" boxing—as it's about the culture of the 1950s, a young girl's involvement with her father's younger brother, who is a middleweight boxer.

> One of the things I liked about Sugar Ray Leonard was that, like all great boxers, he was most dangerous after he'd been knocked down.

My favorite story of my own that involves boxing is "Golden Gloves," very much about the intense, obsessional role of "combat" in the life of a man.

On Boxing *was initially published, in a much smaller version, in 1987. Has there been anything about this book that has surprised you?*

I've been truly surprised by its longevity, and by what one might call its evolution. I'd originally envisioned it as a large book of striking boxing photographs by John Ranard, for which my spare text would be a complement; I had not imagined it in the form in which it is today, an extended sequence of essays, both analytical and memoirist. The initial Ecco Press edition was published in 1995, and contained Mike Tyson material not present in the original. This new edition contains Muhammad Ali and Jack Johnson material not present in the original. Of my numerous books, *On Boxing* seems to occupy a special space, for there are people who have read this book, and have said that they like it, very much, who are not, one might say, readers of "literary fiction"; individuals, mostly men, some of whom remind me of the men with whom my father was acquainted, long ago in upstate New York, as if, through some mysterious evolving, I have come full circle and can now memorialize in prose what, as a child, I could only have felt in the most inchoate and nonverbal of ways. ❧

> ❝ Of my numerous books, *On Boxing* seems to occupy a special space, for there are people who have read this book, and have said that they like it, very much, who are not, one might say, readers of 'literary fiction.' ❞

Have You Read?
More by
Joyce Carol Oates

MISSING MOM (2005)

Nikki Eaton, single, thirty-one, sexually liberated, and economically self-supporting, has never particularly thought of herself as a daughter. Yet, following the unexpected loss of her mother, she undergoes a remarkable transformation during a tumultuous year that brings stunning horror, sorrow, illumination, wisdom, and even—from an unexpected source—a nurturing love.

"A powerful, moving and unpredictable novel." —*Atlanta Journal-Constitution*

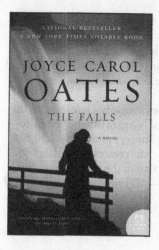

THE FALLS (2004)

A man climbs over the railings and plunges into Niagara Falls. A newlywed, he has left behind his wife, Ariah Erskine, in the honeymoon suite the morning after their wedding. "The Widow Bride of The Falls," as Ariah comes to be known, begins a relentless, seven-day vigil in the mist, waiting for his body to be found. At her side throughout, confirmed bachelor and pillar of the community Dirk Burnaby is unexpectedly transfixed by the strange, otherworldly gaze of this plain, strange woman, falling in love with her though they barely exchange a word. What follows is their passionate love affair, marriage, and children—a seemingly perfect existence.

But the tragedy by which their life together began shadows them, damaging their idyll with distrust, greed, and even murder. What unfurls is a drama of parents and their children; of secrets and sins; of lawsuits, murder, and, eventually, redemption. As Ariah's children learn that their past is enmeshed with a hushed-up scandal involving radioactive waste, they must confront not only their personal history but America's murky ▶

past: the despoiling of the landscape, and the corruption and greed of the massive industrial expansion of the 1950s and 1960s.

"With inimitable virtuosity, Oates weaves the still potent lore of Niagara into her extensive narrative. Using imagery of the river and falls as a driving force, she creates a seamless and engrossing flow that in the end seems natural, inevitable."   —*Washington Post Book World*

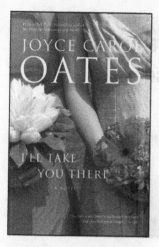

I'LL TAKE YOU THERE (2002)

Anellia is a student at Syracuse University, and away from home for the first time in her life. Headstrong, vibrant, and occasionally obsessive, she embraces new experiences with a headlong enthusiasm for life and love. In her quest to belong Anellia discovers the risks and rewards of confronting the world so passionately.

"Oates knows few contemporary rivals for her expertise at conjuring up the frenetic compulsion of forbidden desires."
—*New York Times Book Review*

Have You Read? *(continued)*

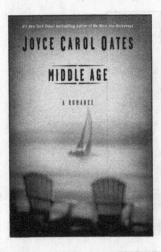

MIDDLE AGE: A ROMANCE (2001)

When Adam Berendt collapses suddenly, his death sends shock waves through his home town, the affluent hamlet of Salthill-on-Hudson, New York. Its inhabitants are beautiful, rich and middle-aged, and, following the demise of Berendt, suddenly forced to confront their own mortality and morality in this richly comic study of middle-class mores.

"A magnificent treat. . . . *Middle Age* is the work of a master in her prime."
—*San Francisco Chronicle*

FAITHLESS: TALES OF TRANSGRESSION (2001)

In this vibrant collection of twenty-one stories Joyce Carol Oates explores with sympathy and unsparing insight the darkest territory of the human psyche. A startling look into the heart of contemporary America, *Faithless* tracks the interior lives of men, women, and adolescents caught up in erotic, forbidden, and mysterious adventures of life-changing significance.

"Again and again [Oates] finds new language to describe the immensity of desire. . . . She twists back against our assumption, seeking always the grisly pop of revelation."
—*New York Times Book Review*

Have You Read? *(continued)*

BLONDE (2000)

Blonde is the deeply moving exploration of the inner life of the woman who became Marilyn Monroe and a portrait of American culture hypnotized by its own myths. Poetically sensual and compulsively readable, it traces the destruction of a cultural icon, but never loses sight of the real woman behind the invention.

"Ms. Oates has hit another one of her targets. This vengeful history is about the majesty of imagination. Marilyn's self-imaginings were cruelly curtailed. Comes now the artist to accord Marilyn her rightful status, as artist. The artist uses flesh and fact, the artist transcends them." —*New York Observer*

Don't miss the next book by your favorite author. Sign up now for AuthorTracker by visiting www.AuthorTracker.com.